LIVING PROOF

Clebe McClary
P. O. Box 535, Pawleys Island, SC 29585
(843) 237-2582

email: clebe@clebemcclary.net
web: clebemcclary.net

Acknowledgements

Many have contributed to making my life a "Living Proof." I would not be writing this book without the loving support of my family, Deanna, Tara, and Christa. To my parents, Mr. and Mrs. P. C. McClary, Jr., a special thank you. Both have gone to be with the Lord, but I will never forget their love and guidance. Thank you to my mother, Jessie, who unselfishly gave of her time. Whether it was Boy Scouts, church functions, Little League practice, football games or track meets, she was always there. Thank you to Daddy, "Mr. Pat," for teaching me how to hunt and fish and for teaching me how to work. Most of all, Mother and Daddy, thank you for teaching me how to love people, whether they're woodcutters from Hell Hole Swamp or bankers from Wall Street.

Thank you to my sister Virginia, for her love and nurturing of me in my early years. She gave me a great appreciation for many things, including travel, history and reading. Virginia and her husband, Norbert J. Delatte, were educators for 29 years with the Department of Defense military schools, teaching the children of men and women in the military. They are now retired and living back at the old homestead in Georgetown, South Carolina. Their three sons are: Norbert, Jr., a top honor graduate from the Citadel and MIT, now a professor at the University of Alabama. He and his wife Lynn and daughter Isabella live in Birmingham. Patrick, whom I swore into the USMC upon his graduation from the Citadel, is a lieutenant colonel and a helicopter pilot, currently stationed in New River Air Station, Jacksonville, N.C., accompanied by his wife Kimmy and their daughter Rachel and son Mark. Paul, a graduate of the University of South Carolina, is a professional chef and makes his home in Orange, New Jersey with his bride Janka.

Thank you to my sister, Patty, for her example as a leader, as President of the SC State Student Council,

Governor of Girls State, Candidate for Girls Nation and SC Teacher of the Year in 1987. Patty still teaches eighth grade at Fort Mill Middle School in Fort Mill, South Carolina. Her husband, Billy Barron is a ranger on the Anne Springs Close Greenway in Fort Mill. They also have three children; daughter Vereen teaches third grade. She and her husband, Mike Brown, live in Fort Mill with their daughter, Taylor and son, Ken; Bo is employed by Leroy Springs, Inc. at Springmaid Beach. He and his wife Debbie live in Georgetown with their three daughters, Joni, Ashley and Hailey; Mary Gin is the traveler in the Barron family. She teaches fifth grade in Hailey, Idaho.

A special thank you to all of my teachers and coaches. Thanks especially to my first coach, Bill Dufford and to John Smith, Charlie Thompson, J. C. Hudson and Chick Gainer for teaching me how to live on and off the athletic field.

Thank you to my friends, life's greatest treasure, for making Living Proof worthwhile. Thanks to Dean Fowler, Jr., Dr. Conyers O'Bryan, Dr. Jim Boatright, Billy Barron and Norbert Delatte, my brothers-in-law, and each a special part of my life.

To the memory of Kenny Brady and Kent Bramlett, who were almost like sons to me. Even though their lives were brief, they were worthwhile.

A very humble and personal thank you to all veterans of WWI, WWII, Korea, Vietnam and the Gulf War. Thank you for giving what it takes.

To order books or tapes or to contact regarding speaking engagements, call 843-237-2582 or write to:

Clebe McClary
P. O. Box 535
Pawleys Island, SC 29585

ISBN 0-9640666-2-9

Reprinted 2002 by Sheriar Press, Myrtle Beach, South Carolina

About the Author

Can a young Marine, body shattered by the weaponry of modern warfare, rebound and turn personal defeat into personal victory? Lieutenant Clebe McClary recounts his courageous story of rebuilding his devastated life. During his tour of duty in Vietnam he suffered the loss of one eye, his left arm, and subsequently underwent 33 operations to retain usage of the remainder of his body.

Today Clebe McClary is in the service of the Lord's Army, traveling the world over, attesting to personal faith in Jesus Christ. His life shows that he genuinely embodies a personal vow which he took upon entering the Marines:

"Any mission assigned will be accomplished in a superior manner, no matter what the obstacles."

About the Co-Author

Dianne P. Barker was a columnist for the Johnson City (TN) Press-Chronicle where she worked for nine years as a staff writer before "retiring" to begin a new career as a mother. Her story on the last Tennessee soldier to die in Vietnam won the Associated Press Managing Editor's Award in 1973. A graduate of East Tennessee State University, Dianne attended the School of Christian Writing, sponsored by *Decision Magazine,* in which she had a feature published. She is author of the book, *Billy Graham in Big Orange Country,* and also Harold Morris' life story, *Twice Pardoned,* the best selling Christian book in 1987. She and her husband, James make their home in Johnson City, Tennessee.

Table of Contents

Dedication

Affectionately Dedicated

To my darling wife, Deanna
My Precious daughters, Tara and Christa
whose love is a constant challenge and
a daily inspiration to me.

In Loving Memory to Goggie—

Home with Our Lord
on Super Bowl Sunday

and Ma-Ma Willis
A True Prayer Warrior
Now Home with the Lord

To our parents:

Mr. and Mrs. Pat McClary
Mr. and Mrs. Dean Fowler
for always understanding and caring!

Each of these loved ones has truly been willing to
Give What it Takes!

Foreword

Clebe McClary represents all that is good in America. He grew up as an all-American boy who loved sports and had big dreams and ambitions.

This is the story of what happened to the dreams and aspirations of a promising young athlete when his country called him to serve. The reader will have the opportunity to share in the sad moments as well as the happy times.

Clebe's tremendous courage is an inspiration to all who have read or heard his story. I am privileged to have known him personally and can call him "my friend."

What Clebe discovered in his own life is available to you. It will never be clearer than it will be in his story.

Thank you, Clebe for allowing me to share in a piece of your life.

Tom Landry
Coach of the Dallas Cowboys 29 years

Clebe with Tom Landry at the FCA National Conference in Williamsburg, Va.

To You Dear Clebe

To you dear Clebe, I write this with pride;
For it's men like you fighting side by side;
Who make this world a better place to live,
But oh! what a price you had to give;
From hippies to yippies and draft dodgers too,
I'm sure it made fighting lonely and blue —
We can't replace your eye or your hand,
Or the miserable days you had in Japan,
But one day there will come on this lonely shore
A Savior so great, who will say "Suffer no more."
This world will end its worry and strife;
And to you dear Clebe, there will be eternal life.

by Annette Fowler Boatright
Clebe McClary's sister-in-law
Charlotte, N. C.

Introduction

Clebe McClary is my friend. He is a man who has been greatly used of God. I want you to read his story because you will be moved to tears and to a greater dedication to God. Clebe has spoken several times, and on each occasion he has touched our people and received a standing ovation.

Clebe personifies the message I preach. It is good to know that the power of God at work in his life will work in the lives of others also. Clebe is a living testimony that God answers prayer.

Clebe stands for old-fashioned patriotism. I am proud to have a friend who says with me, "I love America."

Clebe was injured many times in Vietnam and left for dead. Somehow he survived and returned to the United States. He has had over 30 operations and suffered much physical damage including the loss of an arm and an eye. In all this Clebe did not become bitter. He paid no attention to the protesters who ridiculed him for fighting in Vietnam.

After returning home, Clebe came to know Jesus Christ as Savior. His conversion was dramatic and life-changing. Ever since his conversion Clebe has had a radiant smile and a positive testimony for Jesus Christ. He says he would fight again for his country. He wore his uniform proudly and defended Americanism. Clebe is a hero — I like to call him a champion for Christ.

We have been in several patriotic rallies together. I have heard his testimony several times and each time renew my allegiance to the United States of America. When Clebe testifies how he was near death, I am grateful for every young man who gave his life that we might be free. I will admit that I often shed a tear when I hear this young man preach.

This life story is the living proof of the power of God. Everyone should read this book. It will encourage you in your walk with God. My prayer is that God will give us more champions like Clebe McClary.

Jerry Falwell

Medal of Honor Recipient (Posthumous) Private First Class Ralph H. Johnson, Charleston, SC K.I.A. March 3, 1968.

Many gave much, Ralph gave all.

I

Oh, God! Not Me!

I have chosen thee in the furnace of affliction.
Isaiah 48:10b (KJV)

Gunships peppered the hilltop with rockets just before we dropped in. The helicopters circled and hovered briefly as we stood ready to kickout windows and return enemy fire if necessary.

The patrol- my nineteenth with the First Marine Division's First Reconnaissance Battalion- was a relatively unknown area behind enemy lines in the Quan Duc Valley about thirty miles south of DaNang. We were to prepare the way for a mammoth operation involving several thousand troops.

The routine warning order had been given by our planes. They had dropped leaflets and used loud speakers to tell the Vietnamese civilians where we were going and where they could find food and shelter. If the North Vietnamese Army (NVA) came across the leaflets, they customarily either vacated the area or built up such a strong offensive that we earnestly wished we were somewhere else.

My team of thirteen men- several on their first patrol- proceeded to land on Hill 146, set in a lush valley southwest of An Hoa where our planes and helicopters were based. Another recon team had visited the hill months earlier. Our routine overflight to survey the area before the patrol may have given the enemy an idea that we would be coming. They set a death trap.

The choppers stirred up dirt on the summit, uncovering three powerful box mines as well as booby traps and a pungi pit. The mines were concealed in wooden boxes about the size of a shoe box, with wires running underground to a hill about one hundred and fifty yards away. There, a handful of enemy troops probably awaited our arrival, hoping to pull the wires to set off the mines and blow up the choppers.

Pfc. Tom Jennings jumped out and cut the wires to the mines, discovering one was a dud, but either of the others could have blown us to bits.

The hill was about the size of a football field. At one time it had been a small tea plantation, so its slopes were terraced into almost a perfect staircase on all sides. Rocks and bushes provided very little cover so that it was vulnerable to attack. We wasted no time setting up our defense. I helped the men place our claymore mines, booby traps and trip flares. Then I began clearing the pungi pit- a treacherous rectangle measuring roughly four by six feet wide and six feet deep. The walls of the pit were cut amazingly straight in ground that seemed as hard as a brick. A plaited mat, attractive enough to hang on the living room wall, served as a trap door concealing bamboo stakes sharpened and covered with human waste that would cause infection if one fell in. Bamboo poles, leaves, grass and rocks covered the mat, but the choppers knocked off enough dirt to spoil the camouflage.

Using the mat to form a lean-to, I took my kabar (a heavy casetype knife) and chiseled a notch in the side of the pit near the top, large enough to sit in. My radio man and corpsman dug a foxhole to my left, and three other men settled in a foxhole to my right. The remaining eight took cover about fifty yards behind me in a crater that had been carved by a 2,000-pound bomb. We were in the best fighting position that my team had ever had. Now the waiting game began.

The enemy must have watched every move we made. We kept a low profile and talked little, intently scanning the valley. Shortly the North Vietnamese made their presence known by an eerie strategy- beating sticks together and chanting. The activity was intended to wear down our nerves while we dodged sporadic sniper fire. On the second day a rifle bullet just missed me. I responded by calling in artillery fire. That night an attack by the enemy on An Hoa sent up fireworks reminiscent of a Fourth of July celebration. As a result, the operation planned in our valley was cancelled, and we were to be picked up. However, bad weather prevented choppers from coming as scheduled. That delay would affect the rest of my life.

Our third day on the hill was quiet — a quiet more unnerving than the noise. A few rockets and mortars hinted at a coming assault. We appeared to be surrounded.

Darkness clamped down with smothering suspense. None of us slept. We were on 100 percent alert, each man in position, posed for a deadly encounter, nerves taut, ears strained to hear the slightest sound. . .

In the hush of midnight, I heard a rustling noise at the bottom of the hill. Was it the enemy moving or talking? Did my men hear it too?

I inched out of the pit toward the three men to my right. As if my move were their cue, the NVA launched a frenzied attack with small arms fire, hand grenades, and satchel charges.

Struck immediately in the neck and shoulder by a grenade, I dived back in to the pit and radioed for artillery and air support for our position. At the same time a suicide squad — a sapper unit of about a dozen enemy-charged up the hill. Grenades, with pins pulled, were tied around each waist and held in each hand. They exploded and killed the NVA as they attempted to destroy us.

My men fired furiously. I had nearly emptied my shotgun when suddenly it was showdown. An enemy soldier hovered right above me. I got off the first shot. He lurched forward, plunging into the pit with me. A satchel charge in his hand exploded, hurling both of us through the air like limp rag dolls.

Man, where's my shotgun! I reached back with a bloody stump . . . my left arm ripped off below the elbow.

Oh God! Not me! My thoughts screamed into the infinite blackness. I lay stunned, unbelieving.

This nightmare . . . let it end!

A shriek from my men to the right- an enemy grenade had been lobbed into their foxhole. One dead, another fatally wounded.

To the left, my radio man and corpsman were unconscious . . . maybe dead. In the bomb crater were five wounded.

Fight or be slaughtered! Unsuccessfully I tried to pull grenade pins with my teeth. To bolster my men I darted from one position to another, directing fire. Another grenade soared in.

My face! Blinded by blood, I didn't suspect the left eye was blown out. I choked on blood and broken bits of teeth . . . my lips and gums burned. I couldn't hear. My hand throbbed.

The bomb crater! My only chance! Then another grenade . . . my legs shredded!

Sensing movement near me, I lay motionless, pretending to be dead.

It's all over now!

An enemy soldier stepped over me and aimed his weapon at my head but the shot pierced my neck instead. A few feet away another enemy stuck an NVA flag into the ground, marking his conquest.

Then I was alone-my body racked with pain, my mind in agony that my team was about to be wiped out.

Deanna . . . in days we were to meet in Hawaii. Would I ever see her again?

It seemed that hours passed as I lay on blood-soaked enemy soil in the shadow of death, longing as never before in my life to live. God-Christ-Heaven-Hell-these thoughts never entered my mind.

If only I could get my men off that hill alive . . . if only I could see my wife one more time . . . The blackness of death seemed near. My mind drifted back to my coaching days at Florence, South Carolina, and my first meeting with Deanna.

Clebe and Deanna, Okinawa, Japan, 1999

Deanna McClary, Pawleys Island, South Carolina

II

Barefoot Beauty

Who can find a virtuous woman?
For her price is far above rubies.
Proverbs 31:10 (KJV)

While grading test papers in the Florence gym one night, I remembered that one of my football players had wanted me to hear his combo play at the opening of the Florence Mall. Not taking time to change, I put on sweat pants and jacket, jumped into my convertible and arrived at the Mall just as one of the Moore Junior High cheerleaders, Annette Fowler, was getting out of a car.

"Coach," Annette said, "I want you to meet my sister, Deanna."

I guarantee that was the best-looking sister I'd ever seen- a teeny bopper in Bermuda shorts and knee socks!

Seven years younger than I, Deanna was a cheerleader at McClenaghan High. I had paid little attention to the cheerleaders because I did a lot of scouting instead of attending our home games. When at the games, I usually stayed in the press box; therefore I never noticed Deanna. Now I decided to get better acquainted. I doubted that she would give me the time of day, which happened to be October 6, 1965, her mother's birthday. Deanna had driven Annette to the Mall to hear the band while she shopped for a gift. I thought she was as snobbish as she was beautiful, walking off after the introduction. But hers is a different story.

Deanna:

So THIS is the coach everyone in town is wild about! He is not good-looking . . . he's absolutely beautiful! This strong, rugged, slim, brown, athletic man/boy . . . he looks like the statue of a Greek god. And his smile! So real that it's almost unreal! This is foolish, acting silly over a junior/high school coach. He doesn't look it but he must be a million years too old for me. I wished I were older as we exchanged the usual "nice to meet you" greeting and went our separate ways to hear the band perform. (I forgot Mother's gift).

I tried to look interested in the band, but my eyes invariably fell upon "Coach." Maybe I was imagining it but every time I looked at him, he seemed to be looking at me. I felt a blush.

A senior football player came over and asked if I had met "Coach."

Oh, yes!

"Let's go over and talk to him. Okay, Dea?"

"Well, okay."

Clebe was friendly and easy to talk to. I kidded him about his being a showoff, wearing his letter sweater with all of his awards on it. He must have lettered in everything, but he was actually humble about it all. I was impressed more than ever, trying to play it cool. Then the band finished and Clebe returned to the gym to finish grading papers.

After he left, Annette and her friends surrounded "Big Sis" bubbling with enthusiasm about "Coach" and me. To satisfy their curiosity, I told them that I was dating "Coach" Saturday night. When they began jumping and hollering "Yippee" all over the Mall, I confessed I had been kidding. What if they went to school the next day and told Coach what I'd said! He'd think I was bananas!

Clebe:

Not convinced that Dea was kidding about the Saturday night date, some of the fellows warned me that she was a snob.

"You can't touch her with a ten-foot pole," they insisted. "That's not the kind of girl you want to date."

Oh, but I did!

On Sunday afternoon after scuba diving, I called Deanna and asked her to have dinner with me and go to a movie. Being beautiful and popular, she never lacked dates and usually scheduled them two weeks in advance. She never accepted late dates . . . but she accepted mine.

I almost blew my chances by arriving 45 minutes early and catching her in a robe, barefooted, and her hair in curlers. She looked like "good golly" but she still looked pretty good to me! Moments later, she appeared as elegant as a fashion model.

Deanna:

A sophisticated date with a coach!

I tried to act anything but 17 as we went out for seafood at the Gang Plank Restaurant. When our dinner was served, Clebe suggested, "Let's say the blessing."

I bowed my head, closed my eyes and waited . . . and waited . . . and waited. When on earth is he going to pray? I wondered. Embarrassed, I finally asked, "Well, are you going to pray?"

"I already did," he said. "I was waiting for you to finish!"

I could have died! I never dreamed he meant silent prayer. He started to laugh, and I figured I'd blown it.

Later, in the movie I was so nervous for fear that he might want to hold my hand and even that would go wrong that I hardly remember the film at all. Clebe did hold my hand, and it was perfect. He was in every way a gentlemen. He took me home promptly and did not try to kiss me on this first date. That made me feel very special.

He had strict principles, as I did, and I felt at ease around him.

Clebe:

Deanna and I began dating almost every weekend. During the week I sent her letters and poems from school by Dea's sister, "Annette Express." Many of our dates were at the gym where Dea made giant posters with encouraging slogans for my athletes while I prepared for games or cleaned the gym afterwards. Our big date was dragging the track. Dea drove my Mustang with the drag attached to smooth the surface while I followed on foot to check the surface. She also served as my scorekeeper at meets.

Deanna:

Watching Clebe work taught me some valuable lessons about dedication and perseverance. He had such concern for his students, yet he was a strict disciplinarian. More than once he made athletes get their hair cut before a game. No hair cut, no being on the team, he told them. Still they adored him. His advice and example developed stamina and character.

In December, Clebe popped the question.

"Will you wear my ring?"

His class ring . . . go steady . . . I panicked!

I did love him, but I still liked other people too.

"I know I'm asking a lot," he went on. "This is your final year of school with parties and proms . . . so much going on. I don't want to cause you to miss it all. But I would like for us to go together."

Going steady seemed serious. Reluctantly, I told him, "Clebe, I would love to, but I don't think I'm ready yet."

He didn't push. "Okay. Just take the ring, and whenever you are ready, put it on and tell me."

In a few weeks, I did just that!

I wanted to see Clebe more than ever, but his schedule was too cramped for much time with me. He ran daily, so I began running with him so that we could just be together.

In the early morning, he jogged five miles from school to my house to see me before I left for class. I'm sure my mother's pancakes and sausages were an added allurement! The whole family loved Clebe. My sisters Annette and Jennie and brother, Dean Jr., treated him like a brother. My grandparents, Goggie and Paw Paw Fowler, thought he was such a fine boy. Grandmother Willis was happy for us.

When the time came to meet the McClarys I was nervous. Driving from Florence to Georgetown, it seemed we would never arrive at Friendfield Plantation. I felt at home immediately, welcomed warmly by his parents, receiving a "bear hug" and kiss from his dad, "Mr. Pat."

After a delicious meal prepared by Mrs. McClary and Marie, we talked all afternoon about hunting and plantation life. As we left I wondered what the McClarys really thought of their college-graduate son dating a high school student. I was relieved when Clebe later shared with me a letter from his Mom: "Clebe, we think Deanna is a fine girl. She is sensible, mature and intelligent. Your Dad especially likes her better than any other girl you have brought home because she likes to talk hunting."

Clebe:

A teacher-student relationship being somewhat touchy, we kept our dating low-keyed, spending a lot of time with her family and mine. While I enjoyed being with Dea, I had no intentions of getting too "serious." I planned to coach a swimming team at Myrtle Beach during the summer and to enter graduate school at the University of South Carolina in the fall. I had been offered a fellowship that would enable me to work toward a master's degree in psychology while coaching some under Paul Dietzel. There was no time in my life for marriage.

Since we weren't supposed to be together at school functions, I passed up the junior-senior prom. Deanna invited one of her old boyfriends to be her escort. I decided to tell her of my plans for the future and suggest that she date other boys.

Deanna:

I was crushed! I had fallen deeply in love with Clebe and thought he was in love with me, but now he wanted to break off. Once I had bought an imitation diamond ring and told our friends that we were getting married. It was only a joke, but I had thought that someday it would be real. Now I wanted to hide from the world. At first I refused dates with other boys, but soon I decided to "chin up" and enjoy life as Clebe appeared to be doing.

About this time I was asked to be in the "Miss Florence" pageant. Clebe wrote to wish me his best, even though he did not approve of my entering and used it as another reason to end our relationship . . . he didn't want me on public display. I was chosen first runner-up and later elevated to "Miss Florence" when the winner relinquished her crown to go to Europe.

One day a friend, Ed Cribb, invited my family to eat at Olivers Lodge where he was manager. He introduce me to a tall, handsome young man named Ken who reminded me very much of Clebe. Ken sat with me while we finished our meal then we walked out on the dock behind Olivers to look at the ocean and a lovely full moon. Just then a green Mustang convertible drove up and out bounced Clebe McClary! Ed called him over to the dock and Clebe seemed to choke on his words as we mumbled our hellos.

"How do you like our new boyfriend?" my littler sister Jennie teased.

"Fine! Good to see y'all," Clebe managed. Adding that he had a date, he drove off. Those words stabbed me. I realized it really was over for us.

I dated Ken, unaware that he planned to room with Clebe at the University of South Carolina in the fall.

Clebe:

That summer I coached the Waccamaw swim team composed of athletes from Myrtle Beach Air Force Base and the cities of Myrtle Beach and Conway. Among the 35 swimmers, ages six to twenty-eight, were a Brazilian who won a Bronze medal in the 1956 Olympics in the butterfly competition and a ten-year-old, Lee Proctor, who became a national record holder in the free-style 50 meter.

I dated other girls but missed Deanna. When I heard that she and Ken were becoming serious, it knocked some sense into me. I must have been out of my mind to let her get away! Going to Florence to see her, I found Dea cordial but distant, afraid of being hurt again. Insistent that we remain just good friends, she began going with me to swim meets and on picnics. Walking on the beach beneath a shimmering moon began to work its magic.

On July 26, the ocean glittered like silver as we strolled in the breakers. I had a belated graduation gift for Dea and a special place to present it- the old Huntington Castle. Guiding her over the sand dunes and shushing her lest the night watchman think we were vandals and shoot, I helped Dea up to the flat roof where I gave her a book on the plantations we had visited together.

Deanna:

I ripped into it, eager to get this over with and leave before the mosquitoes caused fatal injury.

"Oh, thank you Clebe," I hugged his neck, swatting a dozen mosquitoes from my face. "Now can we please go?"

He kept talking and twisting my birthstone ring on my left hand.

I was getting angry- standing on that spooky roof with all the bugs in the world mad at us and Clebe still talking. I wondered why he seemed to be so nervous.

Suddenly, he was saying,"Well, will you?"

Will I what? I wondered.

Then I looked at my hand and saw a ring sparkling as my birthstone never did! What was it he talked about while I pretended to listen? While I worried about the bugs, he had asked me to marry him!

"Please, let's go down, Clebe. I think I have malaria already!"

As he helped me down, my thoughts did somersaults. Think about your heart and the pain he put you through, my mind screamed. Say, yes! yes! my heart pleaded. I knew that in college Clebe had been engaged to a girl, but she had returned the ring. He traded it to Ed for scuba diving gear. Now he had bought another ring. Could I hurt his feelings?

"Yes, I'll marry you!" sealed with kisses.

As we walked back down the beach to his car, I asked him to repeat the proposal because I hadn't listened the first time!

Clebe:

We announced our engagement to Ed and "Miss Teeny" at Olivers Lodge that night, and Dea proudly displayed the diamond for her Mother and Aunt Gee Gee on the beach the next day. Laughing, they asked, "At what dime store did you buy that ring?" They knew I had jilted her once and didn't believe we were really engaged. The dime-store diamond she had worn before was bigger than the one I gave her!

"This one's for real," I assured them.

Dea wore the ring to bed at night but left it off during the day until she decided for sure that we should spend the rest of our lives together. A few days later the decision was obvious by her smile as she ran up the beach at Myrtle Beach Air Force Base during a swim meet. I ran to meet her, kissed her, and reached for her hand with the ring as the men clapped and cheered and the rain started to pour!

III

Molding a Marine

The Lord is with thee, thou mightly man of valour.
Judges 6:12b (KJV)

My future was settled — graduate school of the University of South Carolina, a teaching and coaching career, and marriage to the girl of my dreams. On a Georgetown street one day that summer I related my plans to a friend.

"Clebe," he said, "have you been in military service?"

He probably didn't mean to embarrass me or to imply that I had to serve but his question started me thinking. In teaching, I realized how great an influence a teacher or coach can have on a young person's life. I knew some who apparently entered the profession only to receive a military deferment. I didn't want to be ranked with them.

In two months I would be beyond the age requirement for the draft, yet I felt an obligation to my country. Turning down the fellowship at the University of South Carolina, I enlisted as a private in the U. S. Marine Corps.

All of my life I had thought about becoming a Marine. As a child I listened to the adventures of Sgt. J. C. Marlowe, mother's cousin, a career Marine from Murrells Inlet. I remember his collection of photographs, particularly those of Korea, which gave me a love for the Orient and a hope that someday I too, would visit there. I could not have imagined then in what capacity I would make that trip.

The disciplined military life appealed to me. The Marines' "Esprit De Corps" agreed with my ambition: "Any mission assigned will be accomplished in a superior manner no matter what the obstacles."

Arriving at Parris Island in September, 1966, I was chosen for officer training and sent to Quantico, Virginia, for ten weeks. On Good Friday, March 24, 1967, I was commissioned a second Lieutenant in the U. S. Marine Corps and assigned to the Basic School and Quantico for 21 weeks of advanced training.

On Easter Sunday, March 26, in a lovely formal wedding at First Presbyterian Church in Florence, Deanna and I pledged our love and joined our lives.

We had barely said "I do" when the first argument of our marriage erupted. Reaching the steps of the church on our way to the reception, Dea looked at my convertible then at her gorgeous gown and announced, "I'm not going to ride in that thing with the lid down. I'll ride with Daddy."

"If you ride with Daddy," I replied, "you'll be with him from now on." She went with me, her hair and veil blowing in the wind.

Our car was painted and decorated from one end to the other; cans dangled behind and rocks rattled in the hubcaps. We were quite a spectacle driving the 60 miles to Camden, South Carolina, where Dea's uncle, Sam Fowler, had promised us the honeymoon suite at his Holiday Inn for as long as we wanted it.

I carried Dea across the threshhold then returned to the car for our luggage.

"Need a little help?" came a voice behind me . . . J. B. Lovett, Dea's cousin. He and his girlfriend had thought it would be fun to pay us a surprise visit.

"Get out of here," I growled. I had planned a cozy steak supper for two in our room- four definitely was a crowd!

Deanna:

After supper in bed, we watched TV and called home to thank our parents for everything. Then I went into the bathroom to change into my new long white nightgown. Aunt Gee Gee supposedly had kept my bags safe from intrusion . . . I couldn't believe what she had done! My gowns were sewn up and tight and all sorts of funny items were stashed in my suitcase. I ripped the stitches loose and emerged in the white gown, feeling like a queen.

The next morning Clebe jogged five miles while I dressed for breakfast. Then we drove to Asheville, North Carolina, where we would tour Biltmore Estate and go hiking. We had stopped on the way to visit every coach Clebe knew; I thought he surely was proud to show me off! But I hoped we didn't meet anyone while I was dressed in mountain climbing garb.

Suddenly Clebe developed a severe toothache. Agonizing for him, I watched out the window, hoping to see a dental office. What do you know! One right in front of us! He insisted that I go in with him. It was no coincidence that Clebe knew Dr. Bill Mynatt and that the toothache disappeared as mysteriously as it supposedly had come! He invited us to dinner but we declined, explaining that any time other than the second night of our honeymoon would be fine. More than two was still a crowd!

We spent the rest of our brief honeymoon in the beach house owned by my parents at North Myrtle Beach. It was a romantic ending . . . newlyweds snuggled before a crackling fire, listening to the roar of the ocean, and looking ahead to a storybook life.

Clebe:

An apartment in the officers housing complex at Quantico was our first home. Dea, mature for her 19 years, was the perfect wife, making a happy home for our "family," which included a beagle puppy that we gave ourselves as a wedding present and named Easter for our wedding day. While I plunged into war training, Dea took some classes at Mary Washington College in Fredericksburg. She made friends quickly, especially with the neighborhood children with whom she spent hours playing baseball, making cookies, singing, and talking. One night, the kids rang our doorbell and asked, "Sir, can your wife come out to play?"

Deanna:

When we returned to the plantation on leave, Mr. McClary gave us a duck and suggested that we have some of the other officers over for supper. Equipped with Mrs. McClary's cookbook dealing with wild game, I went to the commissary and bought the necessary items to prepare a feast. We sat down to dine in elegance by candlelight . . . our best china and silver, with flowers sent by the officers.

Suddenly Clebe noticed the bulging duck, grabbed it and ran into the kitchen.

"Clebe's carving," I explained. "He'll be back in a minute."

When he returned, the duck had not been carved yet looked considerably smaller.

"Clebe! What have you done to my dressing!" I shrieked.

"Is that what that was?" he breathed a sigh of relief. "I thought Marie had forgotten to clean that rascal's insides!"

I thought he was kidding and had just scraped it into a bowl as a joke. But he had read about new brides who cooked a turkey with the gizzard wrapped inside. Positive that the duck hadn't been cleaned properly and that I had cooked it never knowing the difference, he held it over the trash can and shook it good.

"Hasn't your Mama ever given you dressing and duck?" I demanded.

"Yeah," he agreed, "we had a lot of dressing and duck, but Mama put the dressing in a bowl, not in the wrong end of the duck!"

Clebe:

The Basic School at Quantico included training in many areas, from military law to combat efficiency. I really worked hard to earn high scores. The day of the physical readiness test, the temperature was near 100 and humidity about 98 percent. I was leading the entire platoon on the three-mile run, carrying heavy gear, when just 300 yards from the finish line, I collapsed with a heat stroke. I got up and ran another 10 yards then fell again. Someone poured a canteen of water in my face, and I tried a third time then went down again. It was like a dream . . . I couldn't imagine seeing the finish line and not getting there.

An ambulance on stand-by duty rushed me to the base hospital where I was packed in ice in an effort to lower my temperature from 108 degrees; not a muscle flinched. An hour passed and still I showed no response. As arrangements were being made to transport me to Bethesda Naval Hospital, I roused, yelling, "I love the Marine Corps! Don't kick me out! Gung ho!"

Those years of physical conditioning helped save my life; the doctors said that had it not been for my strong heart, I might never have pulled through. The heat stroke prevented my playing end on the Marine Corps football team and almost kept me from going to Vietnam. The doctors feared the tropical heat would be too much for me, but I wanted to go and requested that my orders not be changed. I hadn't joined the Marines with the idea of getting out of anything- not even duty in Vietnam. I didn't go to win a medal or to be a hero. And as for glory- there was no glory to win.

Deanna:

During those few weeks following Clebe's graduation from the Basic School, we had time only for each other. We picnicked on secluded islands, storing up memories to see us through the lonely months of separation. Too swiftly the moments marched toward that longest night when we lay sleepless, wanting to believe in a happily-ever-after ending someday beyond tomorrow.

In the early morning sunshine of October 8, 1967, Clebe whispered to me his love, confirmed it with a kiss, and sped away to the plane. Through the tiny window he waved a last goodbye to his Mom and Dad then traced with his finger a final message to me- I love you.

Clebe:

It was a good flight from Charleston Airport to Atlanta and on to Dallas and San Francisco. Reporting to Travis Air Base, I began a new chapter of my life. I walked proudly beneath the sign reading. "Through this door march the world's greatest men" and boarded a jet for the long flight to Indochina.

Our stop in Hawaii was brief; there was no time even to leave the airport. I expected to see more of the islands later when Dea joined me there for R & R. By the time we landed in Okinawa, my first foreign country, I had grown weary of looking at the ocean.

I had plenty of time to reminisce of home- Mom, Dad and the delightful days of my childhood. Half-way around the world, my mind drew mental pictures of those I had left behind.

IV

The Plantation

Thou didst possess my inward parts and didst weave me in my mother's womb. I praise thee because I have been fearfully and wonderfully made.

Psalm 139:13-14a (Berkeley)

I was reared on the 10,000-acre Friendfield Plantation just outside Georgetown, South Carolina, where my father served as caretaker for forty-four years. His parents had owned it at one time, but sold the plantation during the Depression. People spoke of it as a "tough break" for our family, but it wasn't for me- I had all the hunting, fishing, horseback riding, and other glorious benefits of outdoor life while the owner, Mr. Radcliffe Cheston of Philadelphia, Pennsylvania, paid the taxes.

Born prematurely in Florence, South Carolina, on November 30, 1941 (a week before Pearl Harbor), I weighed just three pounds and four ounces, an embarrassing size for one with a name like Patrick Cleburn McClary III. My great grandfather, James McClary, Jr., was a Confederate sergeant in the Civil War, serving under Major Patrick Cleburne. The Cleburne coat of arms and family motto means "Forward, the Cleburne's do not know otherwise." He named his son, born in 1867, Patrick Cleburn McClary, who in turn gave the name to his son (my father). I carried the III tag with pride.

At seven weeks of age I came home at Friendfield, having stayed in the hospital until my weight reached five pounds. "Daddy Joe" Vereen, my mother's father who was living with us then, could hold me in one hand. When I fell asleep after a few sips of milk he looked at Mother doubtfully and declared, "Never raise him . . . never raise him!" At times it seemed he might be right. When I ran an extremely high temperature, Mother rushed me to Florence, since Georgetown did not have a hospital. I celebrated my first birthday in the infirmary where I had spent the first seven weeks of life.

Our home was a comfortable frame dwelling of five rooms, two baths, and an office for Dad. It was located at the east end of the plantation about a quarter of a mile from the "Big House" and a mile from our nearest neighbors. It was a happy home in which my two older sisters, Virginia and Patty, and I grew up.

While the men and boys on the plantation respected Daddy (Cap'n Pat), they also feared him. Mother was different. She was a stately woman with a generous, loving heart and gentle spirit. They adored Mother (Miss Jessie), and many of the blacks named their children "Jessie" after her.

The Vereens, Mother's ancestors, were French Huguenots who became pioneer settlers of South Carolina. Her great grandfather, "Pappy" Vereen (Varin in French) was once honored by having General George Washington as guest in his home overnight.

My mother was born on Litchfield Plantation where her father, Joseph Jeremiah "Daddy Joe" Vereen, was employed. At age twelve, she moved with her family to the Bernard Baruch plantation, Hobcaw Barony, where her father managed the farming responsibilities. In 1932 she came to Friendfield as a bride. My father was already working as superintendent of the plantation that had been his home as a youth.

The McClarys, of Scotch Irish descent, were devout Presbyterians who sailed to America seeking religious freedom. They settled in Williamsburg County, South

Carolina, before the Revolutionary War. In 1918 Grandfather McClary purchased Friendfield. He sold the property about 1926 and moved his family to Georgetown, which offered a better education for his seven children.

Radcliffe Cheston, Jr., who bought Friendfield around 1930, turned the plantation into a hunting preserve, primarily for duck and quail. Daddy was one of 17 applicants for the position of superintendent. Mr. Cheston put him to work on a trial basis, cautioning, "You might not suit me."

"That works both ways," Daddy replied. "You might not suit me either."

For the next 44 years, he worked without a contract, nor did he ever have to ask if he had a job the coming year.

Under my father's supervision about twenty-five miles of road were constructed through the plantation. He had the woods thinned, duck ponds dammed up, stables and kennels built, houses for the laborers erected and repaired, canals dug for irrigation, camellias and azaleas cultivated in abundance. A sunken garden planted long ago by slave labor was restored and an avenue of magnolias was planted across the sprawling estate. Rice was grown, but in later years the main crops were hay and oats for the horses and food for quail.

Besides supervising these responsibilities, Daddy trained and groomed the horses and hunting dogs. He also accompanied Mr. Cheston and guests on their hunts, whether for dove, duck, quail, turkey, fox, raccoon, or deer.

Mother specialized in preparing the wild game that Daddy brought in, and friends often came for sumptuous meals prepared by Mom and by our wonderful black cook, Marie. Almost everything we ate was either raised, caught, or shot on the plantation; even flour and meal were ground from our grain.

Gifted at knitting and sewing, Mother made our clothes until we were teenagers. When we bought cow and hog feed at Lawrimore's Feed and Seed Supply Store in Georgetown, Mom carefully scanned the sacks, making sure the colors matched and two had the same pattern, as two were needed to make a shirt for me or a skirt for the girls. At Christmas she found time to make fruitcakes for friends. Etched in my memory is Mother baking for the holidays, surrounded by bowls of nuts and colorful fruits.

During the dreary days of the depression Mother began a tradition that remained the highlight of our Christmas celebrations through the 1950s. On Christmas afternoon all the black families on the plantation gathered in the little church that had been built by slaves on the property. As they clustered around the tree, lit with real candles before electricity was available, Santa Claus appeared (one of the heavy-set black men playing the role convincingly) to distribute gifts. There were presents for each of the children, money for the laborers, fruits for each family, and barbecued pork for their Christmas dinner. Although Mr. Cheston took care of the expense, Mother saw to the details from decorating the tree to purchasing and wrapping gifts.

The disciplinarian in our home was Daddy. A firm believer in the adage, "Spare the rod and spoil the child," he spanked hard with his hand then made us sit on his lap until we quit crying. Even so I preferred a spanking to a "talking to." He didn't favor eating between meals and when I was out with him, I went hungry instead of asking for a snack and receiving a lecture.

I began attending church nine months before I was born and grew up believing in the reality of God. When I was twelve, I was received into Georgetown Presbyterian Church, where my Grandfather McClary had been a charter member. My mother has been church social chairman for about twenty-five years. Daddy, a six-foot, 210-pound Scotch Irishman, said, "Son, join the church," and I joined! Going to church no doubt had much to do with my life and character, but it didn't make me a

Christian, and my joining didn't mean a great deal to me. A personal relationship with Jesus Christ was something I would not find until years later, when thrust against the very gates of hell.

As a child, I had great respect for my father and tried hard to please him. Whenever one of us left home he reminded us, "Remember your raising." He encouraged me, "Son, if you're going to work, work hard. If you're going to play, play hard. If you're going to pray, pray hard. Anything worth doing is worth doing well." He drew from the wisdom of Proverbs, which instructs, "Discipline your son in his early years . . . " (Proverbs 19:18 LB)

My parents administered discipline in my early years. They were strict but loving and fair; they taught by example as well as instruction. I tried to take that teaching with me through life.

Ours was a close-knit family, drawn closer by plantation life. My sister, Virginia, thirteen years older, "mothered" me. I adored her and plotted at age three to crawl into her trunk and go with her to Winthrop College. I was just enough younger than Patty (four- and-a-half years) to be a nuisance, but we grew to be very close. She was an "A" student, cheerleader, and governor of Girls' State as well as representative to Girls' Nation. Blessed with beauty and talent that won her the title of Miss Georgetown, she was successful in whatever she attempted.

As children, Patty and I experienced the normal sibling rivalry. Envious of my long eyelashes, she cut them off. I permitted it only after she convinced me that Roy Rogers' eyelashes were short, too! As we were playing in one of the barns on the plantation one day, she coaxed me into imitating Rogers by jumping from the hay loft onto the back of a horse named "Up and Over," a retired steeplechase participant. At the time I was barely five years old. I jumped, startling the horse, which threw me "up" and "over" into the neighboring mule lot. By the time Patty climbed down the ladder and got over the fence to me, I could move weakly and warned her not to tell Mother! Patty now lives in Fort Mill, South Carolina, with her husband, Billy Barron, and children, Vereen, Bo, and Mary Gin.

Virginia and I shared many interests, including history and travel. In the summer of 1950, after completing her first year of teaching, Virginia took me to see "The Lost Colony," an outdoor drama at Manteo, North Carolina, setting of Sir Walter Raleigh's ill-fated colony. For an eight- year-old, the trip and pageant were impressive, and I never forgot the generosity of Virginia, who spent the money she had earned to provide a special treat for me. Naples, Italy, is now home for Virginia, her husband, Norbert J. Delatte, and sons Norbert, Patrick and Paul.

Norbert Delatte — Top honor graduate from the Citadel Military School, Charleston, S.C. and also MIT with a degree in Civil Engineering. He serves as an officer in the U.S. Army where he is presently completing jump school.

Patrick Delatte — Honor graduate Citadel Military School, Charleston, S.C. — now serving as a pilot and officer in the USMC. Wife — Michelle Smith Delatte and daughter Blair.

Paul Delatte — Youngest brother — graduate of U.S.C., Columbia, S.C. Degree in Criminal Justice.

V

Growing Pains

Jesus grew both tall and wise, and was loved by God and Man.
Luke 2:52 (LB)

Ten thousand acres is a lot of territory for one boy to explore, but I never tired of the adventure.

Mrs. Marie Johnson, who worked for our family more than forty years, assisting Mother with the cooking and cleaning, had twin nephews, Amos and Andy, who lived on the plantation. Together, we roamed the woodlands and trudged the marshes, challenged by the vastness of our little world.

While exploring a barn one day, we came across a box of oblong pills that looked like the cough drops that my granddaddy, "Pa Pa" McClary, had given us when we visited him. I remembered those cough drops and identified the pills as the same. We devoured them eagerly, and they weren't too bad. As we chewed the last of them, the twins' mother found us.

"Oh, Jesus! Oh, Jesus!" she screamed, running down the road to tell Daddy. "Amos and Andy done eat rat poison!"

"Don't worry," he soothed calmly. "They'll be all right, It'll kill the worms and be good for 'em."

"Yes, suh, Cap'n Pat," she added soberly, 'but Clebe eat 'em too!"

At that news, Daddy tossed us all into the truck and sped to the hospital!

Once I acquired a walking cane and pretended to be Mr. Cheston, ordering Amos and Andy to move a stack of wood from one shed to another. Just as they were completing the job, Daddy came up and gave me a spanking that left a 'marked' impression!

There were other youngsters on the plantation from Thanksgiving until Easter when Mr. Cheston's children brought their families. Mr. and Mrs. Antelo Devereux of Philadelphia had two sons, Johnny and Devy, about my age. Mrs. Hugh Fosburgh, New York, had four children: Frances, Harry, Alexandria and Whitney Tower. George Cheston did not marry until late in life; his step-son was killed in Vietnam while serving with the Green Berets.

Occasionally my "Yankee" friends invited me to supper at Mr. Cheston's "Big House." It was everything one would expect a Southern Plantation home to be- a stately mansion set among towering magnolia trees draped with Spanish moss. The spacious rooms were handsomely furnished. We children ate in the kitchen with the cooks.

As a youngster I enjoyed spending the summer at "Sandspur," our beach house at Pawleys Island, about ten miles from Georgetown. I crabbed, shrimped, fished, and sold some live bait.

My first real job was sweeping the fishing pier at Pawleys. I had already been earning a little money by selling live bait, bailing out boats and cleaning docks for our beach neighbors. The boat that I bailed out most often belonged to our next-door neighbor, Mr. Ralph Ford. I lost the job when he caught me filling his boats with water so that I could get paid to bail them out!

My cousin, Herbie McClary, was with us a great deal at Pawleys. He was six months younger than I and as close as any brother could have been. We played, thought, even dressed alike in flannel shirts and dungarees which Mother made. She taught us to swim when we were just little tykes, clinging to her toes as she sat on the dock. She also showed us how to dip crabs from the dock with a net and to dig "keyholes" in the sandbar at low tide for clams.

By the time I was about four, Daddy started taking me with him to work around the plantation. We'd eat a big breakfast and leave about daybreak. By nine o'clock, I was getting into his hair, so he'd leave me with some of the black laborers- David Nettles, James Graham, James McCray, Isaac Reed, Wesley Bright, or Mum Harriett, an old women who was born at Friendfield and lived there all of her eighty-plus years. Dropping me off, he'd head out on the tractor. Not infrequently, he would return home for supper to be met by Mother, anxious to know, "Where's Clebe?"

"Good gracious!" he'd exclaim. "I had him today, didn't I? I left him somewhere . . . I'll be back in a little while."

Hopping into the truck, he'd drive all over the plantation, honking the horn from house to house and hollering, "James, have you seen Clebe?"

"No, suh, he wadn't with you this mornin' when you came by heah."

"Isaac, have you seen Clebe?"

"Yes, suh. I done fed 'im and put 'im to bed. He's in the house. I'll get 'im."

I ate coon and possum with them and slept in just about every house on the plantation! This association with blacks blessed me years later when I worked with black troops in Vietnam.

Almost as soon as I learned to walk, I went hunting with Daddy. My first gun was a double-barrel 16-gauge L. C. Smith which Daddy brought to the hospital when I was born. The gun — a gift of W. H. Truesdell, a wealthy friend with whom he hunted — weighed twice as much as I did!

By age four I was picking up the birds that Daddy shot. When he hunted squirrel I trailed closely, careful to stop when he paused to listen. I would appreciate that training years later behind enemy lines in Vietnam.

At six years of age I first shot a gun, a double-barrel .410 L. C. Smith which Daddy bought. I was just eight when I first shot at- and missed- a deer. I must have missed twenty more before killing one at age twelve. Those were trying years for me, the son of such a successful hunter.

Daddy was about as proud as I was when I killed my first deer. We were in the Wash Hand Ditch Area of Georgetown County. I was kneeling behind an old stump cracking pecans when I heard the dogs running and the bushes shaking. I looked up just as a four-pointer nearly ran over me. I shot it in the head and it fell almost at my feet.

"I got it! I got it!" I yelled. There was rejoicing all around!

After we skinned and cleaned the deer, Harry Parler "bloodied" me, smearing my face like an Indian in war paint, as is customary when a hunter kills his first deer.

James Graham helped me to learn the ways of a hunter. He taught me how to ride a horse and how to listen to the dogs and work them. Daddy couldn't understand why I couldn't immediately do something correctly, but James had more patience. He realized that I had to learn, and he was an excellent teacher as well as philosopher. When good things happened, he observed, "That's a blessed thing."

Our hunting friend, Mr. Parler, who worked many years for Humble Oil Company, was pleased at receiving a raise and wrote to his boss, "As old James Graham would say, 'That's a blessed thing.'" His boss wrote back, saying, "I've looked in Bartlett's Book of Quotations, but I can't find James Graham. Who in the world IS James Graham?"

In the middle of the plantation there stood the remains of a factory which once manufactured fertilizer out of fish. The project had long since been abandoned, but the foundation remained, with walls ten to twelve feet high, making a pool where bullfrogs thrived. Frog legs are a real delicacy, and we had our fill. Each spring and summer, Daddy and I would go frog hunting. He shot the frogs, then lowered me with a rope to the marshy bottom to retrieve them. After devoting years to this sport, I queried, "Daddy, do you reckon there might be any alligators down here?"

"Aw, no, there can't be," he assured me.

Not long afterwards we arrived just as a big 'gator glided into the sunshine. I must have been wading around with him for years.

The 'gators were notorious for killing our hunting dogs; therefore we killed them first if we could. One that we killed had seven dog tags in him. We cooked the meat and fed it to the dogs- sort of turn about, fair play!

One spring day Daddy came along on horseback and spied an alligator in the duck pond nearby. He shot the 'gator, sending it sinking back into the water, and called the workers over from the rice fields to get it out. Several waded into the pond and punched around with their pitchforks. Finally one yelled, "I feel him, Cap'n Pat!" and they lifted him out.

Counting the knots which extend from behind the 'gator's eyes to his nose, Daddy realized that this one was about twice the size of the one he had shot. When it began to kick and splash, the men scrambled up the bank. As the 'gator slithered away, Daddy hollered, "You'll have to go over about fifty feet!" With quivering voice, one of the men replied, "Cap'n Pat, we're through 'gator huntin' this season!"

During my Thanksgiving break from college one year, Daddy and I and several other men were deer hunting on the Esterville Plantation on the inland waterway in the lower part of Georgetown County. A cold snap had formed ice on the ponds, but we had a good hunt. About dark the dogs started running in a rice field at the edge of

Winyah Bay. Daddy saw the deer and shot it, driving it into the rice field.

Giving me a flashlight and a rifle, and attaching one old dog that he didn't think much of to a string tied around my waist, he sent me after the deer. He suggested that I remove my clothes and boots so that they wouldn't be wet and freeze going home.

Stripped to my underwear, I waded into the icy water. The dog trailed the blood quite a distance before I came upon the deer, swimming but in bad shape. I shot it in the head, grabbed it by the horns, floated it out, and pulled it up on the hill. Daddy grinned his pride as two truckloads of other hunters joined us. Seeing me, they guffawed, "Pat, it's dark and freezing cold, but you sent your son out there without his clothes to swim around in the ice after that deer! What's wrong with the dogs in the truck?"

"Good gracious!" Daddy roared. "The dogs would get distemper and die. We can cure pneumonia!"

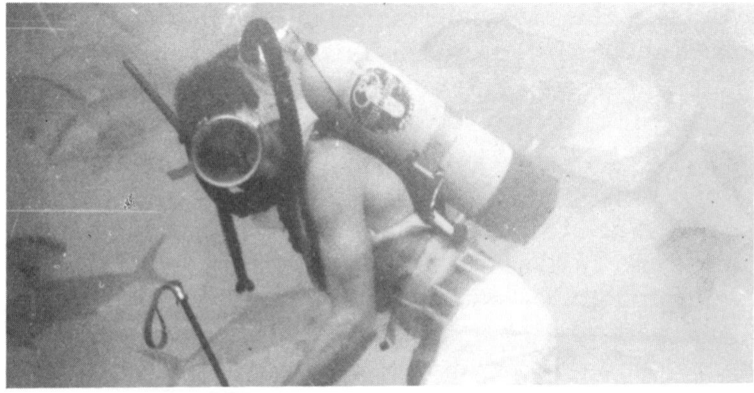

Clebe scuba diving 100 feet down.

VI

Run Your Own Race

In a race, everyone runs but only one person gets first prize.
So run your race to win.
I Corinthians 9:24 (LB)

I loved sports and remembered practically every record in football, baseball, basketball and track. The big radio in our kitchen made Bobby Richardson and Mickey Mantle seem like personal acquaintances. When no one else was around to play, I staged my own baseball game in the back yard, battling along side my radio teammates against another big league team. Pitching the ball against the steps, I called an out if it hit in front of me; if it went high, the batter had a homerun or a triple, depending on where the ball hit. For a boy in the country, a ball and glove provided sufficient recreation; but Daddy complained when I knocked the screen loose from the door!

My first hero was Paul Joseph, a high school football player in Georgetown, who is now a dentist in Camden, South Carolina. I changed my name to Paul. Next I idolized Doc Blanchard, the Army fullback. In Sunday School class, I refused to answer the roll unless my teacher called me Doc Blanchard.

School didn't interest me much . . . I only intended to go long enough to learn to read "funny books." I made

A's in first grade until it was discovered that my "sweetheart," Frances Bellune, was doing the lessons for me! I was halfway through the grade before anyone knew I still couldn't read or write. I could say the alphabet from Z to A perfectly but didn't handle it correctly until about the third grade.

By the time I reached fourth grade I began to suspect that the world was not all good. Ed Cribb and I shared a hobby- collecting full-page color photographs of animals on the back of comic books. We traded books with friends, many times swapping two without a back for one with the nature picture. We had quite a stack when someone stole them from Ed's locker. My faith in mankind suffered another severe setback when a similar experience happened in the sixth grade. Daddy had permitted me to take some Indian Relics, including arrowheads and pottery pieces, which he had found while hunting and riding over the plantation. The display was stolen off the teacher's desk. Those two incidents first illustrated for me the truth expressed in Jeremiah 17:9, "The heart is deceitful above all things, and desperately wicked: who can know it?"

At Winyah Junior High School I came under the influence of Coach Bill Dufford, head basketball and baseball coach and assistant in football. A good man and well disciplined, he encouraged me to achieve in sports.

"Clebe, you're agile; you're fast," he said. "You can probably make it as an athlete; but you've got to be willing to sacrifice, to pay the price."

I was willing. Determined not to drink or smoke, I didn't even drink carbonated beverages from eight grade until late in college. That discipline rewarded me with some successful days in sports.

"It's not the size of the dog in the fight but the size of the fight in the dog," Coach Dufford emphasized. I learned to apply that truth to many situations in life.

At Winyah High, I lettered in football, basketball and track all four years. Coaches Chick Gainer and J. C.

Hudson spurred our football team to a 20-2 win-loss record during my last two years. But along with this record, our team earned an ugly reputation by stealing jerseys from the schools where we played and silverware from the restaurants where we ate. The team became known as "Chick and his thirty thieves."

The boys needed constant supervision, which was an impossible task for any coach. When the coaches were a little late for practice one day, the boys threw rocks, breaking out a number of windows in the school. I never understood this destructive nature and believe it reaped a corrupt harvest in later years. One teammate ended up in prison, some suffered broken marriages, and others failed in business; there were a few success stories. When I went into coaching, I remembered the "thieves" and realized the need for discipline and supervision of the players.

Track proved to be my sport. Our high school team was organized during my freshman year following the annual "Olympics" competition at the school pitting the classes against each other in baseball, volleyball, tug of war, three-legged races, sack races and relays. The event began with a 2-1/2 mile marathon; the winner received the honor of lighting the torch to open the "Olympics." I was one of three representing the freshmen in the marathon.

We started so slowly that I felt as if I were walking. When I began to run, "Sleepy" Brinson, one of the leaders for whom I had great respect, warned me against running fast, explaining that I would tire quickly and be unable to finish the race. Though bored, I followed his advice. With about a quarter-mile to go, everybody started to sprint. In a mad race up the steps and down the hall to the finish line in the gym, "Sleepy" beat me by about a half a step. I'm convinced I could have won had I pulled into a lead earlier. I learned then that you run your own race. I won the event my last three years in high school.

Coach Ted Jacobson, who came from Racine, Wisconsin, to South Carolina for Army duty at Fort Jackson and remained in the area afterwards, watched the marathon and recognized the potential for a track team. He selected six athletes to compete in our first meet at Loris, South Carolina, on a country track- five laps to the mile and a stump in the middle. I was one of about forty boys lined up to run the mile. Coach told me to stay behind until he signaled me to pass. I lingered in sixth place then began passing when Coach advised. On the last lap, I took the lead and won the race.

Having tasted victory, I threw my heart into the sport, determined to receive acclaim as a champion miler. I began running the trails at Friendfield, stopping at intervals to lift weights. Accompanied by the hunting dogs, I cut new trails, with snakes hitting my feet and quail springing out of the bushes.

My strength increased as I worked on the plantation and at the 500-acre farm we owned near Friendfield. In winter I hauled hay to feed the 64 cows and calves at the farm. In summer I helped crop tobacco, combine oats, and poison cotton. In a hurry to play ball one day, I accidentally put weed killer instead of insecticide on 6-1/2 acres of cotton.

Plowing cultivated my ability as a runner. The logging mules kept a good pace and helped me develop a long stride. This exercise, coupled with a strict diet generous in eggs, raisins and nuts, contributed to my success in athletics.

My running style was about as graceful as a mule's. I was really a "mudder" and "gutter", performing better on a wet, muddy track than on one in good condition and winning by fortitude rather than by style. Thinking about a race, I didn't have a great deal of confidence. Deep down, I believed I could win yet feared something might go wrong. I liked to get the lead on the first lap and keep it.

Our track at Winyah was built by the team. The 440-yard dirt track met pole vault and high-jump standards. It was equipped with hurdles, broad-jump pit and concrete slabs on which discus and shot put circles were marked according to specification.

Ed Cribb started running track during our freshman year at Winyah. Besides being my best friend, he was my best competition. Sometimes we clasped hands and crossed the finish line together to share victory honors- and there were many, under the training of Coach Charlie Thompson.

In my first mile competition during my junior year, I faced Moultrie's Leon Parrott, who already had about four races behind him that season, plus another advantage- the meet was on his home ground. The small, sandy track was about five laps around a baseball field with just a line to mark the pole. Each time I tried to pass, Parrott sprinted; I dropped back and he slowed. I started to pass again, but he sprinted until I dropped back. We kept that up for about five laps. Coming off the final turn I sprinted but couldn't overtake him. He beat me by about a step.

We met again a couple of weeks later at the Citadel Track and Field in the Charleston "Evening Post's" Fourth Annual Relays. Since Parrott had beaten me in my first race of the season and remained undefeated in about seven races, he earned the pole lane; I took lane two. I remembered how he had taken the kick out of me on his home track by alternately sprinting and jogging so that I never could get around him. My only hope was to stay beside him or get ahead of him.

We stayed together for the first lap. Unable to get ahead, I determined not to drop behind. Actually I ran a lot further than he did, perhaps 20 yards, staying on the outside lane. Shoulder-to-shoulder all the way, we finished the first lap in about 60 seconds, much too fast for high school runners. We did the same thing on the second lap . . . he wouldn't let up, and I wouldn't drop back. The third and fourth laps were a repeat of the first two. On the last lap, with about 220 yards to go, I got about half a step on Parrott. I knew then that I had him and kept right on going. As we were coming off the curve and down the straightaway I pulled into a 15- to 20-yard lead and beat him with a time of 4:47.8. The "Post" called it a "big upset."

I continued undefeated in the mile through the next year and went on to win the state championship. I also held the Florence Optimist Relays mile championship for three years. I was never a bad sport, but I didn't enjoy losing. I like the way someone put it, "I never lost a game or a race in my life . . . they just ended too soon."

On January 11, 1960, Ed and I began training for our last track season at Winyah. We ran every day except Sunday until the season started in mid-March. We worked out often at the golf course, circling it ten times one day and running the straightaways and jogging the curves and hills the following day. Another day we ran one lap as hard as we could, jogged one, then ran another hard one. We ran an average of 50 to 60 miles per week, occasionally racing from Georgetown to Pawleys Island, a distance of about twelve miles. Wild hogs in the bushes along the ocean route improved our speed! At times we also ran the 26 miles from Georgetown to Murrells Inlet. We loved the beaches and adopted as our theme, "The sun and sea; you and me."

Six weeks of rigid training- sometimes battling wind, rain, and snow- gave Ed and me an edge when the season opened in March. After taking honors at the Greenville "News-Piedmont" Relays, our team headed for Charleston and the "Evening Post" Relays where I broke the mile record by circling the track in 4:43.7. Ed won the 440 and 880. Later he brought our mile relay team from behind in the final lap to win with a record time of 3:39.

Our last high school meet was the state competition at Columbia, where I won the mile with a record time of 4:44.4. Ed was state champion in the half-mile for the third consecutive year, and our team finished second in the state.

Earning 12 varsity letters in football, basketball and track, I was captain of the track team and chosen "most valuable player" my sophomore and junior years. Selected "most outstanding athlete in all sports" my senior year and all-state end in football, I was one of 33 boys in the state selected to play in the Coaches All-Star Game sponsored by the Shriners. I anticipated college offers of athletic scholarships.

Ed Cribb, 4:13 mile and 1:51 half mile, Coach Charlie Thompson, and Clebe McClary at Winyah High School in 1960.

Clebe, on left, handing to best friend Ed Cribb, who brings us on to victory. Photo courtesy of The Charleston Evening Post.

VII

Two Kings in a Castle

Two are better than one; because they have a good reward for their labor. For if they fall, the one will lift up his fellow: but woe to him that is alone when he falleth; for he hath not another to help him up.

Ecclesiastes 4:9,10 (KJV)

Ed and I wanted to continue our track training through the summer and began looking for a place to live near the ocean so that we could run on the beach. I thought of an ideal place- Huntington Castle, owned by Mr. and Mrs. Archer Huntington. The Spanish-style castle was built during the depression to provide work for the blacks on Sandy Island.

The Girl Scouts had a 99-year lease on the castle. Their leader, Mrs. Siau, agreed to our taking a room in exchange for cutting the grass and keeping away prowlers who had been breaking in.

As Ed and I turned off the highway and drove up the concrete road, it seemed like a scene from the movies- palmetto trees surrounding the old castle hugged by thick vegetation up to the windows. We went inside, and picked out a corner room upstairs with a breeze from two sides, and an adjacent kitchen. To reach the roof we scaled the wall by grasping the bars shielding the windows. As we climbed down to a little brick patio below, Ed shouted, "Clebe, there's a snake down there!" With one foot already on the ground, I turned, expecting to see a small snake. The one I met measured about eight feet! I passed Ed on the way up! He found a stick and killed the snake-and 54 more in and around the castle before the summer was over.

We got up about 4 a.m. to run on the sand dunes before reporting for work at Dawson Lumber Company. It was already hot at 7 a.m. when Mr. C. C. Dawson started us stacking lumber. There must have been ten acres of lumber, and he figured it would take us all summer. We ran from stack to stack and almost worked ourselves out of a job. Finishing an area, we asked Mr. Dawson, who was then about 70, "What do you want us to do next?" He directed us to another stack. About 3 p.m. the next Tuesday, 6½ working days after we started the job, he walked out of his office just as we stacked the last board on the yard-about two million board feet of lumber stacked in a week's time!

"Mr. Dawson," I began, "what do you want us to do next?" He started to point out another stack then, somewhat dismayed, concluded, "I reckon we'll have to find you all another job!"

Ed scaled the timbers brought in on the logging trucks (probably the easiest job at the mill) and I spent the summer running the planer mill (no doubt the hardest work).

One boy, Oscar, picked on Ed all the time. Ed took about as much harassment as he could then one day declared, "Hey, there's two of us!" The other fellows really liked that. They'd say, "There's two of y'all!" Nobody bothered us for the rest of the summer. We heard later that when we clocked in that first day, one of the workers asked another, "Who are those two guys?" He retorted, "Aw, just a couple of high school kids. They won't be out there long, just til the sun gets hot!" We proved him wrong by nearly working everybody in the mill to death!

Hired at $1.25 an hour, we cleared $29.39 a week. It wasn't much to save for school expenses. Mother put our money in the bank every week, and we lived on the $4 cash we received for working on Saturday mornings. We caught fish for food and Mother provided eggs and milk from the farm. I hardly spent a dime, but it took practically all of Ed's $4 to keep him in Pepsi's!

About the first of July I told Ed we weren't making enough money and needed another job. It had never occurred to me to get a job that paid more money. Having a lot of relatives in the area, I went to Murrells Inlet where Mother's cousin, Florence "Miss Teeny" Oliver, put me to work bussing tables at Olivers Lodge, a popular seafood restaurant operated by "Miss Teeny" and her husband, Captain Mack.

I received $1 an hour plus 50 cents a day from each of the 12 waitresses. Since Ed cooked breakfast and kept up the castle grounds, I decided to split my pay with him. He was sitting good- half of my money, pretty girls coming to visit, and plenty of free time to run on the beach; but my work was fun, too, and there were fringe benefits. "Miss Teeny," a woman of immense size- most of it heart- worried that we might starve to death and gave me a box every night containing two quarts of milk, hushpuppies and fish- enough to feed almost everybody at the lumber mill!

When one of the busboys failed to show up one night, Ed landed the job and found the work such fun that he said he probably would have worked for free. However, neither of us turned down the $60 a week.

After work Ed and I sometimes went flounder gigging. Carrying a lantern along the creek banks, we speared the fish with a gig that had prongs resembling a pitchfork. We fried some of the flounder for breakfast and sold some at Olivers. That gave us an idea-we would gig frogs and supply all of the restaurants in the inlet. It looked to be a successful venture until the legs started jumping out of the skillets and the cooks vacated the area!

Ed and I really enjoyed life during that busy summer. When I left August 15 to play in the All-Stars game in Columbia, Ed left the lumber mill to work fulltime at Olivers and moved from the castle to a room at the lodge. He bussed tables at night and spent the days with Captain Mack on his fishing boat. In the fall Ed entered the University of South Carolina, staying until his junior year when he returned to a fulltime job at Olivers. I also worked there intermittently from 1960 to 1965. On Labor Day, 1965, as Ed and I were clearing tables, I looked at him and he looked at me with the same thought. I voiced it: "We ain't come too far, have we?"

Ed learned the restaurant operation well and later went into business for himself. He and his wife, Jean, have several restaurants — Chesapeake House north of Myrtle Beach, Chestnut Hill, Wayside, Drunken Jack's, Santa Fe Station and Marlin Quay.

A few years ago, Ed and Jean drove me to Philadelphia to give a devotional talk to the Eagles professional football team at game time. About 2 a.m. in his motel room, I prayed with Ed for assurance of his salvation. He and Jean now serve on the board of my evangelistic association.

Dr. Jerry Falwell, pastor of Thomas Roads Baptist Church, Lynchburg, Virginia, has said, "If there wasn't a hell to miss- and there is- and if there wasn't a heaven to make — and there is — just having Christian friends and fellowship make being a Christian worthwhile." I feel that way about my friendship with Ed. Many of the best experiences of my life I owe to him. He is aptly described in the wise words of King Solomon in Proverbs 18:24, "A man that hath friends must show himself friendly: and there is a friend that sticketh closer than a brother."

VIII

Purpose in Every Step

So I run straight to the goal with purpose in every step.
1 Corinthians 9:26a (LB)

Offered partial athletic scholarships to Clemson College, the University of South Carolina, Citadel, Florida State University, and Furman University, I chose Clemson at the encouragement of my coaches and my father. I was fairly successful in cross country, winning meets at Wake Forest, Duke, North Carolina State, Citadel, and Georgia Tech.

But one semester at Clemson convinced me that I was neither the athlete nor the scholar I had imagined myself to be. Finding it difficult to work, make good grades and pursue athletics, I decided to make a fresh start at a smaller school. In February, 1961, I transferred to Erskine, a small Associated Reformed Presbyterian College in Due West, South Carolina. Determined to earn my own way rather than to depend on Daddy for support since I had left the school of his choice, I entered Erskine not having enough money for my freshman tuition. Dr. J. M. Lesesne, Erskine president, told me not to worry. He and Mrs. Lesesne were very hospitable; their door literally was always open, and I often slipped into their kitchen late at night to make a sandwich.

I worked hard at Erskine both in and out of the classroom. Asked to accept a work scholarship, I held various jobs, from delivering inter-campus mail to distributing clean linens to the students in the dorms, chauffeuring students and faculty to and from the college, and filling the cracker and drink machines. There was no need to worry about my consuming the merchandise . . . I must have been the only person on campus who abstained from soft drinks!

During the summers, I worked at Olivers Lodge and the Wayside Restaurant at Murrells Inlet. I also took a job with Diamond Construction Company, a Jacksonville, Florida firm building a bridge spanning the Waccamaw River outside of Georgetown. I catwalked beams four to eighteen inches wide, balancing beams across my shoulders about 90 feet above the water.

Since Erskine did not have a track coach or an organized team, I trained on my own, motivated by the success stories of Olympic champions Herb Elliott, Murray Halberg and Bob Richards. I studied the methods of the famous Australian trainer, Percy Wells Cerutty, who invited me to train at his International Athletes camp at Portsea after graduation. However, I declined the offer of a fellowship, not feeling qualified to train with athletes of the caliber of Cerutty and his proteges.

During my sophomore year I went overboard on a health food fad and let my weight drop to about 130 pounds by eating foods rich in vitamins but largely omitting carbohydrates, which are energy suppliers. Competing in the Florida Relays at the University of Florida in Gainesville, I collapsed on the track. The doctor at the school infirmary gave me a huge bottle of vitamins and a jar of peanut butter. In spite of that incident, the track coach, Ray Graves, offered me a scholarship. The physical education director at Erskine still uses me as a bad example.

I ran all four years at Erskine and hitchhiked to meets throughout the country. I collected several trophies by winning at some small school meets and cross-country meets, though I didn't set the world on fire by establishing records. I received the cross-country championship award for 1963-64 at Erskine.

I did not accomplish everything I aimed for in athletics, but I probably developed my body to its full potential. I did not possess the natural ability to be a great athlete. Someone with more ability, following my rigid training, could easily go to the Olympics; but the years I devoted to physical conditioning were not wasted, as I would learn later on.

I received my bachelor of science degree from Erskine during the summer commencement program of 1964. At the Honors Day program for seniors, the Erskine faculty recognized five students by presenting awards for scholarship (the Young Ring); service (the American Legion award); and helpfulness to others (the Algernon Sydney Sullivan distinction). Recipients of the awards were selected by the faculty by nomination and secret ballot. Dr. J. Calvin Koonts, head of the Department of Education and chairman of the Division of Teacher Education, nominated me for the American Legion award and spoke in my behalf. A few years later I returned to Erskine to receive the Alumni Algernon Sydney Sullivan Award also.

Dr. Koonts' graduation gift to me was the McClary coat of arms. He also presented me with a framed letter of invitation from Percy Wells Cerutty, the noted Australian coach with whom he had arranged for me to have further training in cross-country. Although I turned down the offer, I appreciated his letter:

> It has been brought to my notice, and I must commend you upon your singular success as a student, athlete, coach, leader, and as an indefatigable worker, and above all, your excellent personal character. It is this last, of course, that will be your most valuable asset.
>
> It is such, Clebe, as yourself, who can go on to produce first class scholars, and athletes, who in their turn become first class citizens. Therefore, I look to you to be one of those who will advance the world-need in the humanities, and which to me, embraces all aspects of human activities and well-being.
>
> Do, then please accept, not only my genuine interest, and congratulations, but my very best wishes for your future. And accept, also my very real belief in your gifts, your capacities, and your assured success in your work. And, believe me to be, very sincerely in friendship.
>
> Sincerely,
> Percy Wells Cerutty.

My career as an educator began at Dixie High School in Due West where I coached football with Dusty Oates during my last year at Erskine. After graduating, I remained at Dixie High another year, teaching physical education and psychology and coaching basketball, football and track. During my first year there we were upper-state champions in track and football.

During my second year at Dixie, I was teaching a science class when two men from Florence called me out of class. Boone Aiken, banker, and Henry Sneed, educator, were looking for a coach to work in the Florence school system. Accepting the position, I worked with two schools, teaching physical education and coaching football, basketball and track. I led McClenaghan High's "Yellow Jackets" track team to win their first championship in the eight-year history of the Optimist Relays.

In my spare time I went scuba diving with Bill Brown and Henry Smith. Bill, owner of Brown Memorials in Florence, is now a member of my board. Henry was an underwater demolitions expert in the Navy before becoming an electrician in Florence. He miraculously survived electrocution, losing his left arm and right leg; but his attitude greatly impressed me. As we prepared to dive into the ocean, I sometimes needed a hand from Bill to hook up my equipment. Henry never asked for help. He put his tank on, buckled his weights, and got out of and into the boat without assistance. His swimming expertise and breath control were unbelievable; he could stay under the water longer with one tank than I could with two.

We had many good diving days exploring ship wrecks such as The City of Richmond, The Hector, and The New Wreck. The City of Richmond had sunk in a storm as it was being pulled from the Chesapeake Bay to the Bahamas where the boat was to be made into a motel. We found a few so-called treasures such as forks and knives.

Since being wounded in Vietnam I have not been able to dive much because it hurts my ears and gives me vertigo. My first time out with Henry and Bill after my recovery, Henry decided to have some fun. In his sandwich supplies, he found a bottle of catsup and suggested that we pour some over the stump of his arm and leg and my arm stump to see how folks at the dock would react. We appeared to be a bloody mess as Bill pulled the boat up to the Georgetown dock. When several boaters came over asking if we had caught many fish, Bill replied solemnly, "No, we didn't catch many fish. The sharks were bad out there today. Look at these two fellas!" The screaming was terrible . . . people fainted all over the dock!

Lt. McClary with Vietnamese Villagers

Our Church, 1st Recon Chapel, in Vietnam in 1967

IX

Not the End of the World

Thou hast enlarged my steps under me, that my feet did not slip. I have pursued mine enemies, and overtaken them: neither did I turn again till they were consumed.

Psalm 18:36 & 37

Vietnam I found to be a picturesque land where we might have enjoyed spending our honeymoon. Impressive mountain ranges formed a backdrop for the fertile coastal plain that once made this tropical country a leading exporter of rice. Seasonal winds called monsoons gave South Vietnam two seasons- a wet, hot summer from April to November, and a cool, drier winter. This struggling republic in Southeast Asia, bordered by Laos and Cambodia to the west and the South China Sea to the east, measured roughly 67,000 square miles, meager space for its 16 million people.

Small of stature, with dark hair framing faces golden in color, the Vietnamese were warm and patient people. They worked hard in spite of much physical suffering from disease as a result of poor nutrition and sanitation.

The Vietnamese villages were made up of small settlements called hamlets, usually tree-shaded and situated near a river with the rice paddies nearby. The houses, called "hootches" in GI slang, were simple huts with bamboo sides, thatched roofs, bamboo windows and doors, and dirt floors. Furnishings were scant, perhaps a table and some small cots.

The people were friendly, saluting our officers and smiling to communicate as if there were no language barrier. The children let American troops know right away whether they liked them by rating them on a scale from one to ten. If they held up one finger, that was super; ten meant bad news!

The undeclared war- a controversial conflict which cost the lives of 56,000 U. S. troops- was well under way by autumn of 1967 and military activity was picking up, particularly in the northernmost section of the country where I was assigned to the I Corps Division.

The Da Nang runway seemed almost too small for the Braniff International jet as we set down about 3 a.m. October 14, some 13 hours ahead of South Carolina. Flares piercing the darkness and mortars and rockets hitting the airstrip did wonders for my prayer life!

New troops slept on canvas cots in tents set up at the end of the runway, and I was scared. However most of the rocket-like noise proved to be only F-4s breaking the sound barrier. I was glad to see daylight. Jeeps took us up to the base area for the First Marine Division's First Reconnaissance Battalion about five miles from Da Nang.

Base area was a small village within itself. Temporary quarters were provided for the enlisted men in large tents with concrete floors. They later moved to better facilities in hootches accommodating 30 or so men each. These were constructed about three feet off the ground with plywood walls and tin roofs; they were cool, comfortable, and dry.

As battalion headquarters for the First Marine Division in Vietnam, base area was home for the General, as well as the S-2 and S-3 offices where patrols for the entire division were planned. Three companies -A, B, and C- operated from here, as well as a motor transportation unit. I was assigned to 3rd Platoon, Company A. A chopper pad served double duty as a football field and handball court. Meals in the mess cabin were hot and tasty- but nothing to compare with Mom's or Marie's home cooking! At

Freedom Hill between base area and Da Nang was a shopping center with PX and a theater. A hospital battalion was headquartered there, but we had a first-aid hootch at base area.

I settled in the hootch I was to share with six other officers and then went to the Officers Club. The next morning I located a Vietnamese woman to cut the sleeves off my utilities. We couldn't understand each other so I made a scissors motion with my fingers. Shaking her head, she then did sewing motions. I realized that she meant if I would cut, she would sew. I whacked them off, and she sewed them up. Score one victory over the language barrier!

It is customary for new arrivals to be de-briefed and assigned by the General, the head of I Corps who was responsible for all Marines in that area. Some teams were in heavy fighting which kept the General occupied for about a day and a half. When I saw him he needed lieutenants in Recon. During training my request to serve in Recon had been rejected because there was not sufficient time for the additional schooling required.

When the General asked for volunteers, I ignored the memory of my wife's pleas to stay out of Recon and volunteered. The General impressed me as he told us what kind of work we would be doing, what he expected of us, and how to treat the Vietnamese, although Recon had little dealings with them.

I was issued my weapons and combat equipment before reporting to Col. B. C. Stinemetz of Oregon. He was everything one would expect a Marine colonel to be- built like a Greek god, his bearing commanding respect. He talked to me as a father to son and became a good friend. He cared about his troops. While they were in the bush, he stayed by the radio and called gunships to assist them; upon their return from patrol, he met them and commended them for a job well done. At base area he joined in basketball and volleyball games with the men.

At our first meeting Col. Stinemetz was upset. I listened with him to the radio report from the ambushed Texas Pete recon team: three killed, 13 wounded. When the team was brought back, I accompanied him to the hospital where he interviewed those who were able to talk. One of the dead was a gunnery sergeant named Alowine from Texas. I had met him on my first day at the base as he was blacking his face, preparing for the assignment to the Garden of Eden. The team had set in, come under enemy fire, and received orders to return along the same trail they had come. In the subsequent ambush, the sergeant's legs were blown off. A grenade lay beside his mangled body. Two others were killed as tragically. The team fought well, killing 18 to 20 Viet Cong (VC); the men who survived the patrol became my best.

I collected the belongings of the dead and wounded to send to their families.

My hootch provided many of the comforts of home. The other officers and I purchased a small Japanese-made ice box to cool juice and soft drinks. We each had a small private area with rack (bed) and room for a few items. My shotgun and helmet hung on the wall in a handy spot in case we were mortared at night.

Displayed on the walls were pictures and post cards of South Carolina scenes sent by Mother and Dea. Bill Brown sent 14 underwater photos made during the last scuba dive on The City of Richmond. At my request, South Carolina Governor Robert E. McNair sent a state flag "to serve as a reminder to those South Carolinians serving away from home that our thoughts and best wishes are with them."

X

Thorn in the Enemy's Side

Or what king, going to make war against another king, sitteth not down first, and consulteth whether he be able with 10,000 to meet him that cometh against him with 20,000?
Luke 14:31 (KJV)

Recon (short for reconnaissance) was known as a synonym for suicide. This unit, which I consider the Marine Corps' best, operated behind enemy lines. It was made up of a small team of men playing a dangerously sophisticated game of hide and seek.

We worked the territory within a 45-mile radius of base area and became a thorn in the enemy's side. We had to go no further than the first hill to fight. Helicopters transported us to and from our assignments in the mountains and jungles where we spent from four to twenty-six days conducting reconnaissance and surveillance operations to detect enemy troop movement or possible arms infiltration. Our purpose was to gather information- the enemy's location, situations, actions, number of troops.

Some patrols were little more than a leisurely walk in the woods; but most of our forays were 'close calls' with our team just a heartbeat from death, saved by the miracle of timing.

I found that recon teams either completed their mission safely or were badly hurt. Seldom was there middle ground. Confrontations with the enemy occurred with dreadful results. We killed only when we had to and avoided contact as much as possible.

The enemy had several names, the most familiar being "Charlie." The Viet Cong we encountered were mostly farmers by day and fighters by night; they wore coolie hats and black pajamas. The North Vietnamese Army (NVA) regulars were hard-core Communists totally dedicated to their cause and ruthless in their methods. Their soldiers reportedly had been taken from home at about age ten and placed in training camps where they were conditioned to the doctrines of Communism and warfare. Outfitted in khakis, they were equipped with A-K 47s and A-K 50s, excellent Communist-made weapons which have a distinct sound. Hearing that sound, troops sometimes turned and shot. One American sergeant was killed by his own men in this manner.

The Communists used a program of terror and brutal torture. An 18-year-old girl was skinned alive and nailed to a tree; 40 children were maimed by cutting off their hands to keep them from going to school. Entire villages were burned; and the civilians, who were hiding in little safety tunnels under their hootches, burned or suffocated when the VC came through with flame throwers. People were beaten to death with lead pipes; women were sexually abused; and bodies were mutilated and dragged through the villages. In the city of Hue 9,000 civilians were slaughtered by the enemy.

Upon my arrival in Vietnam, I learned that an estimated 600,000 enemy troops had infiltrated our area within six months.

Before assuming command of the thirty-man platoon, Texas Pete, I completed three patrols as a regular trooper. The first took us into the Viet Cong-infested Hep Duc region. Movement was extremely slow in the dense jungle where trees towered 150 feet, forming a canopy so thick that we couldn't see the sky. We came across a trail which appeared to be freshly used, indicating VC in the area.

Three enemy walked along the trail, passing within inches of us as we crouched in the thick undergrowth. Calling a fire mission to clear any VC from the area ahead, we began our sweep up Hill 360.

Hostile fire indicated 15 to 20 enemy waiting for us at the top. When they began throwing grenades, we scooted back down the hill to avoid close contact, our mission successful because our purpose was not to take control of the hill but to find Charlie so that guns could be sent later to clean up the area. Coming upon a couple of hootches, we concluded from the bloody bandages and fresh graves that they must have served as a VC hospital. We called artillery to cover our movement and evacuated the area, evading the enemy until choppers lifted us out.

On patrol to Charlie Ridge southwest of Da Nang, we bogged down in mud after jumping from the choppers as they hovered about ten feet above the deck. Being the rainy season, it rained intermittently throughout the day. The deluge of rain gave way to sunny skies and sweltering temperatures of 110 and above. Charlie used the rain and fog to his advantage, digging tunnels before the sun came out; and we put the hurt on him with artillery and air support.

During this patrol some enemy mortar rounds came close to our position; but when we called a fire mission, the mortar ceased. Charlie caused no more trouble.

Returning to base area, I joined Lt. Wade Barrier for a steak at the White Elephant Club in Da Nang. For dessert, I ordered an ice cream sundae, expecting it to be served American-style. The waitress brought what looked like $20.00 worth of ice cream! Everyone in the restaurant seemed to watch her to see who had ordered it! I was too embarrassed to eat more than a few bites.

A few days later I would have welcomed even the ice cream as we ran out of food on another patrol into the Hep Duc region. This time we went with Lt. Nick Shriver's team and found Viet Cong all over the place. We saw hundreds in the area and counted 17 boats in one place, some being loaded with ammunition. Unable to call artillery without the rounds hitting us, we avoided contact. About 2000 meters down stream we called "arty" which sank one enemy boat.

Rain delayed our being evacuated for two days, and by the time the choppers arrived our food was gone. At base area a hot steak supper awaited our hungry team. We had almost reached the mess cabin when the captain asked for a volunteer to eat with the village chief as part of the pacification program to create goodwill and appreciation for American troops.

"Bear," a six-foot- four, 230-pound lieutenant, said, "I haven't eaten in two days. I'll eat with anybody!" The captain prepared him for what to expect.

"He's going to give you a bowl full of rice with some kind of meat. You won't have any utensils and will have to eat with your fingers. Don't clean your bowl completely or you'll offend the lady of the house . . . she'll think she hasn't prepared enough food; but if you don't eat most of it, she'll think you don't like it." Bear understood.

Chowing down like it was going out of style, Bear thought the meal was rather good but wondered what he was eating. He didn't speak any Vietnamese; and even if he had, no one could have understood him because he came from Alabama! Looking out the window, he saw some chickens and concluded that he must be eating chicken pilau- chicken and rice cooked together. To get his point across to the village chief, he started flapping his arms, pointing to the bowl and making a cluck-cluck sound. The chief realized he wanted to know if he had been eating chicken.

"NO, no, no, no!" he said. Pointing to the bowl, he went, "Bow wow! Bow wow!" It didn't take Bear long to figure out what he'd been eating!

As patrol leader, I usually took a 12-man team to the bush. We became known as "Texas Pete and the Dirty

Dozen." Another team went out with Sgt. Young, who received the Silver Star for his performance on the patrol ambushed just after my arrival in Vietnam.

Behind enemy lines we were hunters, stalking a deadly prey. We chased him through impenetrable jungle, hacking our way through and across mile-high mountains, lugging 110-pound packs on our backs, sometimes pulling them behind us through vegetation so thick that we had to crawl.

Using movement as a defensive tactic, we snooped and hid, making it hard for Charlie to find us. When we had to fight, we hit and ran. We neither picked fights nor dodged them. A firefight was sort of like a ballgame: whoever shot the most the fastest won; and whoever got off the first shot lived. A skirmish didn't bother me at the time; but I was a little shaken afterwards, thinking of what could have happened.

Sometimes we were assigned to areas where an upcoming operation was planned, perhaps a campaign to sweep a valley clean of Communists. In a normal war our troops would have kept sweeping and chased the enemy north, killing and capturing them along the way; but this war had so many regulations that we weren't permitted to be too aggressive. Therefore our goals were different. We conquered an area to keep the VC from capturing the city below or to calm down the enemy activity; then we pulled out for another area. It was not the kind of military campaign in which strategic places were won.

Intelligence groups had "sniffer units" that flew over at night picking up the enemy body and campfire odors. From the air, they could locate a whole company of VC or NVA regulars. Their reports, called "red haze read-outs," sometimes indicated thousands of enemy in an area; and a recon team was sent to verify it. I'd rather have just taken their word for it!

Before each patrol I made an overflight of the area in a chopper. We skimmed over the treetops and rice paddies, observing the terrain for a place to insert (land) and another to be extracted (lifted out) from at the end of the assignment. We noted water supply and looked for enemy activity. We also estimated height of the canopy- treetops usually 100 to 150 feet above the deck (ground). Sometimes we could step out of the chopper onto the deck; at other times, we had to jump 10 to 12 feet as the chopper hovered. Since Charlie kept close watch, we flew over a large region, spending the least time in the area of the upcoming patrol so that he wouldn't be ready for us when we arrived.

I prepared for every patrol by studying maps of the territory and reading reports of all previous patrols in the area. As a result of this extensive preparation, I had little difficulty navigating in the jungle. When my men bickered once about our location, I sent one of them up a tree to determine our position; then I called in artillery fire that almost blew him out of the tree. They didn't challenge me about direction any more!

My men test-fired all weapons the day before patrol and again when we returned to base area. A malfunction on patrol could cost us our lives; so I made thorough inspections of equipment, making sure the weapons and tools were clean and the kabars and bush axes were sharp. The weapon I preferred to use was a Model 12 Winchester pump, similar to the shotgun I had hunted with on the plantation. I was skilled and comfortable with it.

In addition to the M-16 rifles, we took one M-14 (an older rifle) and an M-49 (grenade launcher). We also used hand grenades, gas and smoke grenades, claymore mines, booby traps, trip wire, flares, and other ammo, including 50-and 60-caliber machine guns when needed.

Receiving air support from planes and choppers, we also relied on the artillery battalion to fire from land and sea. Since the latter were as much as 40 miles away, they never saw the target but fired according to my directions. At base area we presented them an enemy weapon or flag as a reward and treated them to a steak dinner at Da Nang.

The cost of war in terms of money is astounding. We easily used $1 million worth of ammunition in one night with artillery and air support. Smoke grenades were used to mark positions when we had air support. Red showed where the enemy was; and green told our location; if the wind blew it, we were in trouble.

Sometimes we ran out of one color and had to use the wrong color. If we were in a lot of fire, we broke contact by throwing gas grenades, then putting on gas masks and running through it to hide in the dense foliage. Familiar with demolitions, we rarely destroyed bridges or roads because we needed them more than the enemy did.

The night before we went out on patrol, I gave the patrol briefing and orders, outlining our mission, describing the expected weather and terrain, analyzing enemy strength, location and capabilities, noting "friendly" troops in the area, and detailing our courses of action.

I also discussed the procedure for loading and unloading the choppers. Getting off the bird, the first four men took the left side and the others took the right. Each had his weapon pointed to cover an assigned direction. Then we moved out of the area as soon as possible in case Charlie had observed our arrival. When being extracted, we didn't rush to the chopper. The first man boarding the bird defended the tail end. If we received enemy fire, we shot the 50-caliber machine gun mounted on the chopper and kicked out the windows to fire our rifles as well. My team had a narrow escape once at a landing zone when the men, tired and hungry, rushed to the chopper without proper caution and received hostile fire.

Cleared areas large enough for a chopper to land were certain enemy targets. Charlie sometimes formed a circle around the landing zone and waited for a team to set in. After the gunships and choppers left and the men started to move out, the enemy opened fire; or instead of waiting, he often planted booby traps, grenades, and mines, aiming to blow up the choppers and everyone in them.

Rapelling was less risky because we needed an area only 10 to 15 meters wide. As the chopper hovered 60 to 90 feet above the deck, we jumped out, wrapping the rope around the waist and rear then hooking it through a snap link to make a seat as we slid down the rope, giving Charlie only a few seconds to shoot at us. As soon as we hit the deck, we were equal: Charlie didn't know where we were; we didn't know where he was. We kept moving, kept guessing, and tried to outsmart him.

XI

No Margin for Error

Though an host should encamp against me, my heart shall not fear; though war should rise against me, in this will I be confident . . . For in the time of trouble,
He shall hide me in His pavilion.
Psalm 27:3,5a (KJV)

As the chameleon changes colors to blend with his surroundings, we painstakingly camouflaged our selves to be absorbed by the jungle greens and browns. While we smeared our faces with camouflage makeup sticks, Pfc. Ralph Johnson — a good-natured black Marine from Charleston, South Carolina — grumbled, "Lieutenant, I'm black enough! Why have I gotta put that stuff on me?" It was necessary to dull the shine of the skin. We didn't wear rings that could sparkle in the sun, and even my Marine Corps watch had a black face and band. Anything that rattled had to be taped down. We found that helmets and flight jackets made too much noise in the jungle; a bandana with leaves stuck in it, or a canvas camouflage hat served better. All supplies were painted brown, green and black.

The enemy's disguise was unbelievable. Waiting for us to come by, the VC sometimes buried themselves straight up for 48 hours, breathing fresh air through a straw; or they sat covered in a hole called a "spider trap" for weeks with only a handful of rice to eat.

Trails and roads we used rarely. We followed instead the animal paths or cut our way through the vines and sometimes traveled in rivers and streams. Movement often was slow: some days we traveled several miles and other days, only a few hundred yards.

The order of march placed the point man first to scout for mines and booby traps. He usually carried both an M-79 and an M-14, effective at long range. We changed the point man about every two hours because if he became fatigued and careless, we could all be killed. My position was second, the primary radio man behind me, followed by the "Doc," (Navy corpsman), M-16 riflemen, auxiliary radio man and finally "tail-end Charlie" who covered our trail by smoothing footprints and pulling vines and leaves over our path. If he suspected we were being followed, he set out booby traps and claymore mines.

Walking single file, we were careful not to step on the same rock as every other man in the team. The fourth or fifth man likely would knock it loose and slide down the hill making too much noise as well as suffering injury. If we heard anything, everybody froze. Thumbs down signaled that it was the enemy. Coming to a bomb crater, open place or stream, we stopped and let the first man cover the second man and so on until we all passed safely. When we made noise by hacking vines or cutting trees, we froze and waited to see if Charlie heard and was making a move to reach us. Even putting a poncho on in rainy weather became an art. First, we would remove our boots, then slide slowly into our poncho knowing that the slightest rustle might give our position away.

No smoking was permitted. Although I do not smoke, I sometimes chewed on an unlit cigar as an outlet for tension. We used hand and arm signals to avoid talking aloud and whispered only when necessary.

We were in radio contact with base station (Pal Joey) at all times, making hourly reports of our situation. When we were on the move and during the night, we avoided talking an answered their questions by clicking the handset. A brevity code was used for radio communication in the bush so that if Charlie were listening, he would not learn of our position and plans. One month, the code was basketball jargon. Helicopter was "jump shot'; gunship was "backboard'; landing zone was "court' and so on. The code served well when we were in a secure position; but if we were under heavy assault or ambushed, we dropped the code and called for help. When a hundred VC were after us, we didn't have time to look up the word for VC!

Our patrol orders were prepared at base area by the S-2 and S-3 offices, which kept reports of all previous patrols, maps showing where the enemy was believed to be, and information about what our teams were doing. I rarely disobeyed orders. On one occasion I was told not to go in a certain direction, but we were being shot at from the other three directions and had no choice. It was difficult for the man sitting at a desk with a map to know our exact situation; so in times like that, common sense was required.

Whether we stopped to eat depended on how near the enemy was and what had been happening. For chow break we formed a circle, each man assigned a position. The long-range rations provided for recon patrols included beefstew, chicken with rice, spaghetti, and chili con carne — very tasty and fattening. Sometimes we warmed them with a heat tab which resembled an Alka Seltzer. When lit with a match, it burned slowly; but it gave off a little odor which could be picked up by the enemy. If he was that close, we were in trouble anyway. Occasionally we also used a small bit of the explosive C-4 which burned hot and fast and served best to heat water. We napped some during the heat of the day after chow break; the enemy usually took an afternoon rest too.

Settling into our harbor site (camp) before dark, we placed claymore mines, booby traps, and trip flares around our position to give us ample warning if Charlie hit. On occasion he disconnected our mines and slipped to within a few feet of us to leave Communist propaganda for harassment.

Darkness was our disadvantage, and Charlie knew it. He usually hit around midnight or just before daybreak. Throughout the night we received H & I fire from artillery (harassment and intermittent). This barrage at intervals not only made the enemy a little leary of coming too close to us but also kept artillery warmed up and hitting on target if we needed it to combat an enemy assault. We avoided movement at night — not even visits to the privy allowed. We took turns sleeping, but often we were on 100 percent alert . . . everybody awake. We formed a 360-position (circle) with string running from my leg to each other man's leg. If he didn't return my tug, I'd know his throat had been cut. Lying on the ground beneath the stars, we made friends with the jungle creatures. By morning, the birds and monkeys thought we were one of them. We probably lay side by side with snakes of many descriptions.

Leaving the harbor site after the animal noises of the jungle grew quiet, we moved in a different direction from the day before, traveling for five minutes, then pausing to listen. Sometimes we pinpointed the enemy by his chatter because the Vietnamese did not whisper. They usually knew we were in the area but walked casually past our position as relaxed as if they were going to the PX.

We took prisoners whenever we could for they were a valuable source of information. Sometimes they were captured walking down from the north, carrying rockets to a launching site. After we fed them, many told us whatever we wanted to know — primarily where their ammunition was stored. Some of the hard-core soldiers refused to talk. We never tortured them. Some 600 of the enemy who were imprisoned just outside of Da Nang apparently received better care from our people then they had ever known. When the Viet Cong overran the prison and opened the gates, no one left until the VC began shooting their own.

On a few patrols we used one of the military dogs trained to smell the enemy. Sometimes if the trainer were shot, the dog had to be killed because no one else could handle him. Another disadvantage in using the German shepherds was that their food and water added extra weight for my men to carry.

As we chased Charlie we waged a small-scale warfare against other enemies — insects, heat, and disease. Mosquito repellent kept these annoying pests under control pretty well in the jungle; but leeches attached themselves to the waist, wrists, and ankles unless we tucked our shirts in and tied our pants at the ankles and our sleeves at the wrists. As temperatures soared, we took salt tablets almost daily. On Sunday we took malaria pills. In addition we received the routine shots to combat disease in the tropical climate.

Because there were many teams going many places, my team rarely received as much ammo as requested on my report submitted to the ammo bunker prior to patrol. There was sufficient ammo for the teams to have a mediocre supply; but if one team took everything it wanted, another team would be weak.

While waiting for choppers to take us to the bush one morning, my team went to eat breakfast, leaving our ammo on the chopper pad. Another team came by and took all of our ammo. I couldn't condemn the "thieves" because I probably would have done the same thing. In some ways, it was dog-eat-dog, even among our own troops.

Supplies were also insufficient. Almost everything that I wore or used came from dead or wounded troops. My boots belonged to Sgt. Frenchie Vereen, who received the Navy Cross. It doesn't help the morale to tell a man that he will receive new boots when somebody gets shot. I concluded that the Marine Corps' budget must be lower than any other branch and felt a bit resentful that the Air Force troops guarding the perimeter at base area dressed in new utilities while my men, fighting for their lives in the bush, had to barter and steal to get supplies. We traded enemy weapons and grenades, pungi pit relics and other combat "momentos" to the chopper pilots for utilities.

An Army chopper loaded with weapons, boots, and utilities landed in our area one night; and the pilot left the bird on the chopper pad while he went to eat with us. Top Sergeant Barker saw that as a perfect opportunity to make a supply run. He and a few other men blacked their faces, sneaked down to the chopper, and cleaned it out. The pilot didn't accept the explanation that the VC stole the supplies, but he left without argument. I felt bad about the incident. We needed supplies but perhaps not as much as the men in the bush waiting for that order.

Though his methods were somewhat questionable, "Top" had good intentions. Finding a private in a military jeep at the PX waiting for an officer to return, "Top" used all the authority of his rank and commanded the private, "Go get me a beer." The naive young trooper took off running and barely got out of sight before "Top" cranked up the jeep and drove to the dock in Da Nang. As the ships came in, he told the "Squad," "I've got an extra jeep here that you fellas could use for a few days while on shore leave, if you'll give me a case of steaks." We ate steak for a long time!

XII

The Tough Get Going

Have not I commanded thee? Be strong and of a good courage; be not afraid, neither be thou dismayed: for the Lord thy God is with thee whithersoever thou goest.
Joshua 1:9 (KJV)

My troops were tough. They gave their best. They obeyed patrol orders almost to the letter and pulled us through some life-or-death encounters with Charlie.

I watched teenagers molded into men by the harsh realities of war. The medals they won were earned by gallantry — not the eloquence of the poet's eulogy but the pain and anguish of blood sacrifice.

In my opinion they achieved combat efficiency as defined by the Marine Corps: the ability to accomplish an assigned mission in the shortest possible time with the minimum loss of life and waste of material.

I tried to find office jobs for my men as soon as possible to get them out of the bush. A few months in the jungle were enough for any Marine.

The weeks scurried past, routine but rarely humdrum. Thanksgiving proved a lackluster day for me, but not so for a friend serving with another recon outfit. On a mission south of Da Nang, Pfc. Adrian F. Lopez was shaken awake by a six foot, 350-pound tiger. As the beast began dragging him by the leg, it was shot and killed by a sergeant who was later killed in action. The men skinned the tiger, saving the skin for the General. When a chopper arrived and let down a rope to hoist the skin aboard, the men had to be left behind as the chopper had revealed their position. It then became necessary for them to stay on the move until they could be evacuated later.

Our next patrol took us deep into "Indian country" on a "flip-flop" assignment, taking the place of another recon team in support of a large operation. We recorded 30 sightings of 195 Victor Charlie and 37 VC suspects. Eleven fire missions were conducted, resulting in three VC killed and another 21 probable VC KIA's. We observed smoke from a possible VC harbor site about 1000 meters from us. It looked like Indian smoke signals in an old western movie. By November 30, we were out of food and surrounded by the enemy. We fired and called in artillery, sending the VC scrambling into the jungle. What a celebration for my 26th birthday! I remembered my 25th birthday party at Gee Gee's and my gift, a Labrador retriever with a coat like black velvet, who proved allergic to water and feathers.

A nine-day mission to Blankenship out-post (O. P.) on Hill 452 gave us a break from bush patrols. Now we had bunkers, a few cots to sleep on, weather nice enough to make photos, even newspapers and magazines dropped from an aerial observer. The hill overlooking Antenna Valley was the site of a permanent radio relay station which kept in touch with other troops in the area and relayed messages back to base. The teams flip-flopped, one coming in as another left. Thus the hill was manned at all times, providing protection for the strategic valley in which was located the only coal mine in South Vietnam.

Returning briefly to the base area, I took my men to Freedom Hill to see "The Sound of Music" before we were needed to support an operation northwest of An Hoa. We inserted without making enemy contact, although previous patrols had reported 181 VC sighted in the area. We called for several fire missions and an air strike during the patrol. One night the VC drove seven water buffalo through our position. I had hoped to take a VC prisoner but one of my men botched the plan by throwing a grenade, confirming our location for Charlie and forcing us to move out under a full moon. We were extracted in time to make the Bob Hope show at Freedom Hill. As we flew over in the choppers returning from the bush, the mountain was covered with Marines waiting for the world famous comedian to begin his show, part of which would be included in his Christmas television special.

No schedule of shows was announced because if the enemy had known where Mr. Hope was going to be, they could have hit the shows with rockets and mortars, killing many of our key people. The comedian acted as if there were no danger or fear. He brought a taste of home. At the end of the show, some 10,000 Marines clustered around the hills stood to sing "Silent Night." There weren't many eyes without tears . . . I'll never forget that moment.

Christmas cards and packages from family and friends arrived in abundance. There were fruitcakes and cookies, assorted gifts and good wishes. I gave most of the sweets to my men but tried to answer all the notes because being remembered at this season by folks at home meant a great deal to me.

Letters and tapes from Dea helped to make the separation bearable. She even recorded songs which I played at chapel services. I listened to her tapes over and over, many times awakening during the night to find the recorder still on.

Pilau, the squirrel I befriended before leaving for Nam, chirped a greeting on tape. The others in my hootch said to me, "We knew you were from the country, but it's bad when you start getting tapes from the wild animals!'

For Dea's Christmas present, I sent a painting of us, the work of a Vietnamese artist for $50.

Dea's gifts to me were more practical — a rubber pillow and a lamp so that I could read at night in base area.

My men gave me a nylon Confederate flag with the names of all of the "rebels" in the platoon and the states they were from. I took it on patrol to signal choppers when we saw them over our area. I spread the flag on top of a bush or in a clear spot to mark our location without attracting enemy attention by shooting flares. My men used to say, "What if that's a Yankee pilot? He'll blow us all away or holler down, 'Good luck, Reb!' and leave us!" When the flag became muddy and worn, Pfc. Martin of Ohio got me a new one. I thought that was pretty nice of a Yankee!

Clebe...the outdoorsman

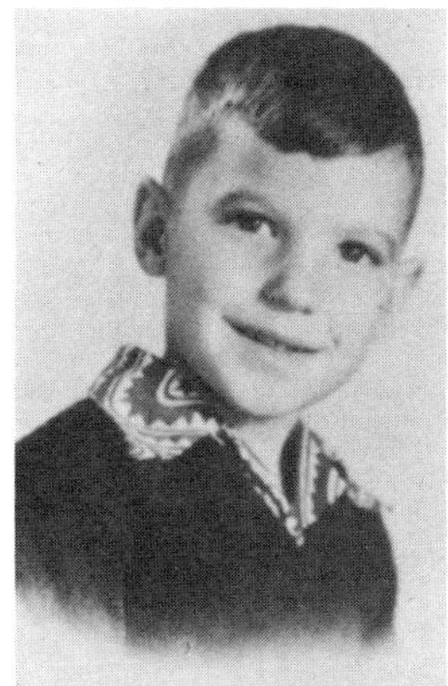

Clebe—first grade

McClary takes baton from teammate Wesley Owens . . . Charleston Evening Post Relays in 1960 in mile relay race.

Winyah High School Basketball
Clebe, Number 20 and Harold Morris, Number 30

James Graham of Friendfield Plantation "My greatest philosopher"

Snowy Small pulled Clebe from frozen pond while duck hunting

Clebe and Dad hunting on Arcadia Plantation

Patrick Cleburn McClary, Jr. at Friendfield Plantation, Georgetown, South Carolina

Two generations, Patrick Cleburn McClary the II and III

Jessie Vereen McClary

Mrs. Patrick Cleburne McClary, III
March 26, 1967

Pat McClary and Maggie

Tom Jennings, Lancaster, PA, killed in action, March 3, 1968.

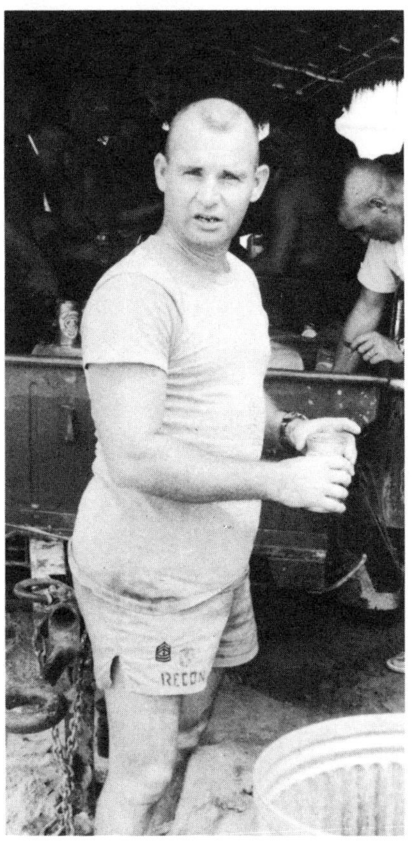

1st Sgt. Otis Barker, Recon Co. A stayed in Okinawa—never came home

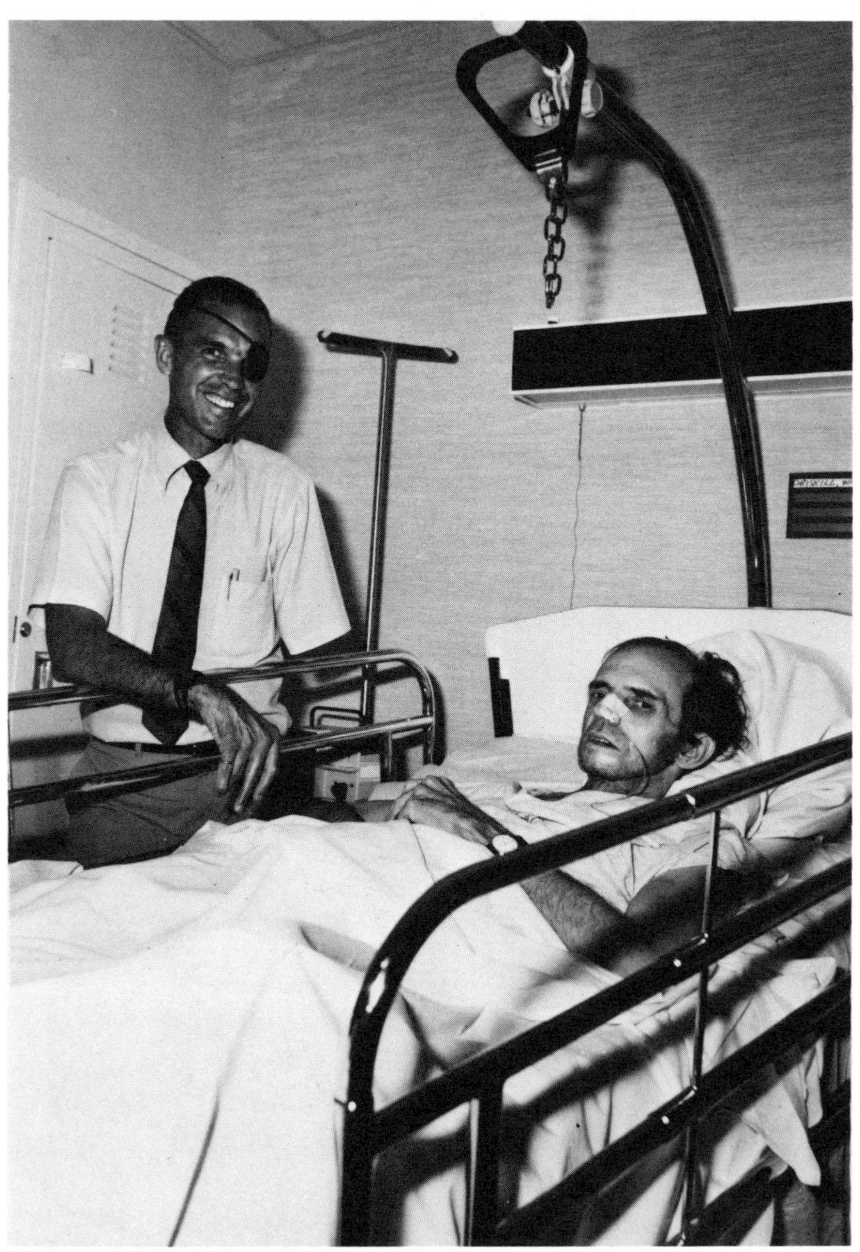

Clebe visiting veterans in hospital

Clebe and Coach Bear Bryant of Alabama, the winningest Coach in Football

by Kenneth H. Cooper, M.D., Founder and Director, The Aerobics Center

RECORD-SETTER PROFILE

Clebe McClary

Age: 44

Hometown: Pawleys Island, S.C.

Date Record Set: Sept. 10, 1985

Physician: William King

Treadmill Time: 36:36

Personal: In Vietnam in 1967 and 1968, McClary was wounded seven times, losing an eye and an arm. Required 30 operations, including surgery for brain tumor in 1981. Motivational speaker. Addresses such groups as National Football League teams about Christian ethics. Runs 2,000 miles a year.

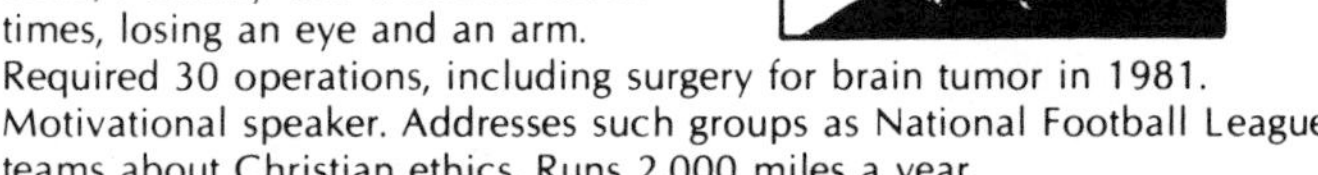

Quote: "I had run all my life, and when I was wounded, my resting heart rate was 36 beats per minute. It took a long time, but I got to where I could run again. I haven't stopped since. I push myself real hard. I get out of my body all I can get."

AEROBICS CENTER BALKE TREADMILL STRESS TEST RECORDS

Following are the current Balke treadmill stress test records for patients of the Cooper Clinic. They are furnished regularly for your information.

MALE			FEMALE	
NAME/PLACE	TIME	AGE GROUP	NAME/PLACE	TIME
Eric Jensen, Texas	33:00	Under 20	Terrie Brown, Texas	29:35
Kyle Heffner, Texas	37:07	20 - 24	Ann Bond, Texas	30:00
Jay Fountain, Texas	35:08	25 - 29	Deborah Strehle, Arkansas	33:02
Norbert Sanders, New York	36:00	30 - 34	Eleonora Mendonca, Brazil	32:10
Jim Ryun, Kansas	36:16	35 - 39	Sharon O'Connor, Colorado	33:00
Clebe McClary, S. C.	36:36	40 - 44	Mary Jones, Texas	29:32
Paul Vernon, Texas	34:34	45 - 49	Anne Zink, Iowa	28:04
Chuck Cornett, Florida	34:36	50 - 54	Ann Radke, Kansas	26:00
Arnie Jensen, Texas	32:00	55 - 59	Patricia Neff, Iowa	24:50
Jessie Santamaria, Texas	31:00	60 - 64	Marion Read, Wisconsin (tie)	21:00
			Ada Campion, Texas (tie)	21:00
George Sheehan, New Jersey	30:02	65 - 69	Constance Hughes, Alabama	21:05
Ralph Osborn, Texas	27:35	70 - 74	Polly Clarke, Colorado	22:00
Johnny Kelley, Mass. (tie)	25:00	75 - 79	Valeira Russell, Texas	17:00
John Clarke, Colorado (tie)	25:00	75 - 79		
Arlitt Allsup, Texas	12:06	80 - 90	Helen Bailey, California	7:30

Clebe McClary, Marine Corp. Marathon time 3:06

The McClary Family at Brookgreen Gardens

Clebe coaching Soccer in Oaklyn, New Jersey

Clebe speaking at the VA Central Office in Washington, DC

Clebe and the boys at the General Store in Little Switzerland, NC

Clebe and Tennis Pro Joe McCleary in Oklahoma City, OK

Clebe at the Gator Bowl in Jacksonville, FL with USC defensive back Bryant "Mookie" Gilliard. In 1984, Mookie had 9 interceptions for the season and 4 interceptions in one game. Both accomplishments still stand as individual Carolina season and single game records.

Dean Smith and Clebe at University of North Carolina

Clebe sharing with athletes before fitness run, AFB, Dover, Delaware

Clebe with Bobby Richardson and Bobby's grandson, Ronnie

Harold Morris and Clebe McClary in Prison, Double life sentence for armed robbery and murder. Harold is the author of Twice Pardoned.

Clebe McClary, USMC, at Vietnam Memorial

Tara McClary and Governor Campbell

Tara McClary, 1992 graduate of Furman University

Christa and her husband, Dr. John T. McElveen

Clebe and Deanna McClary, 25th Wedding Anniversary, March 26, 1992, at home church, Pawleys Island

Relaxing on our day, enjoying a Pawleys Island rope hammock

Clebe, Maggie and Deanna McClary

Clebe and Hans Tanzler, Jr., Mayor of Jacksonville, Florida for 12 years

Clebe with Gen. Jim Kelley, former Commander of the Air University, Maxwell Air Force Base, AL

Clebe with good friend, Chaplain Don Biadog and Col. Jim Farmer of the USMC Jungle Warfare school in Okinawa, Japan

Clebe and General Joulwan in Panama

Clebe, General Kinzer and Deanna in Panama

Clebe, Anita Bryant, and Mayor Hans Tanzler at Rally in Florida. "This lady has guts!"

Deanna and Billy Zeoli, our dear friend who led us to The Lord. Bill and his son Steve produced our movie Portrait of An American Hero.

Clebe with Billy "Z." After all these years, we still thank the Lord for Billy!

Clebe with Chaplain Jeff Watters and
Lt. Col. Thomas Cole at Fort Richardson, Alaska

Young men willing to "give what it takes." Clebe with members of the Texas Aggie Corps of Cadets, College Station, TX, April 1999

Grant Teaff and Clebe at Baylor University

Clebe McClary and Ron Ball, Secretary of Navy

USMC - A United States Marine for Christ

Lt. Clebe McClary, in front of Marine Memorial at the Vietnam Memorial

Clebe McClary in front of Vietnam Memorial Statue

Clebe in Hawaii with Col. Jim Barta, one of the Marine Corps' best. "We swapped last patrols."

Tara—Mesa Verde cliff dwellings

Christa—Mesa Verde cliff dwellings

Clebe and Steve Watson of the Denver Broncos

Tara and Deanna McClary, "Mother-Daughter USA." They will give up their crown in July, 1992.

Tara and Mary Gainey, Miss South Carolina, 1991

Clebe McClary, USMC

Photo by Mexican-American radio man Oscar Munoz.

Lieutenant Clebe McClary in Vietnam, Hill 675, the Tet Offensive, 1968

XIII

Shattering the Sacred

And they shall fight against thee; but they shall not prevail against thee; for I am with thee saith the Lord, to deliver thee.
Jeremiah 1:19 (KJV)

War did not stop the holy season. We were scheduled for a Christmas patrol to the Garden of Eden where our gunships had been shot up as they prepped the area. When my team approached in two choppers, enemy fire struck one, forcing it down. None of my men were hurt, but we had to guard the bird through the night until a reaction force pulled us out the next day. Since the chopper was damaged beyond repair, we removed the engine and radios, then destroyed the remains.

Returning to the Garden of Eden the following day to fulfill our mission, we moved slowly through dense vines and elephant grass eight to ten feet high. We saw some VC suspects bathing in a stream and concluded from their black pajamas and coolie hats that they were woodchoppers. Some were probably enemy because we didn't find that many together unless they were fighting on one side or the other. We observed them for a while but didn't fire because I didn't see any weapons. Four VC walked about 25 meters from us on a trail; since they didn't see us, we didn't pick a fight.

I knew for certain that it was Christmas Eve when two of Santa's reindeer came to within 15 meters of our position — a large doe and a blacktail fawn.

"Good thing it wasn't a buck!" my men teased. "Lieutenant would have had Charlie all over us!"

The Christmas truce started at 6 p.m. December 24. I didn't welcome the 24-hour cease fire because we would have no artillery or air support if Charlie hit- and without doubt, he would. On Christmas Day, the aerial observer flew over and, with a loud speaker, called upon the VC to surrender. He also had a message for us: "Merry Christmas . . . Santa Claus is dead."

We counted 32 woodchoppers walking along a nearby trail. A lot of other people passed, but we saw no weapons. Some women with axes and knives went by, and I suspected they saw us. Later that afternoon a sniper broke the truce by firing about ten rounds at me and my radio man. I got behind some rocks and gave the order to fire. We didn't bother to confirm the KIA's.

It was tough fighting on Christmas Day, but life is not sacred when your own is threatened . . . Christmas and Sundays are not hallowed in war. Mother used to get upset when I went duck hunting on Sunday. I knew she wouldn't approve of my killing people on the Lord's Day, but it was just another day to the enemy . . . our lives were at stake.

To avoid further contact we ran about 1000 meters in 25 minutes. I poured two canteens of water on Pfc. Ford of Texas to avert a heat stroke. After observing in the jungle all day December 26, we were extracted the following day. I recommended that future patrols in this area take 25 to 30 men because a small team could really be hit hard.

I watched the New Year arrive while commanding the reaction force. We were on alert for 24 hours, ready to move out in seven minutes to aid units hit by VC.

Planning a patrol to Antenna Valley which had been the scene of much action, I scheduled 18 men and extra equipment, including the 50-and 60-caliber machine guns. The overflight revealed numerous trails, some resembling highways and others just four to six feet wide. Rock apes and gorillas were also plentiful. We didn't know what was in there, but we went in expecting to meet Charlie and determined to get him.

Right after we landed, Pfc. Jennings located three mines in the landing zone — a "bouncing betty," a regular grenade and a 105-round. If our chopper had set down on them, we would have been blown to bits. I don't know how Jennings found them, but I suspected he could smell those rascals. He often ran point when we were in areas likely to be rigged with mines and was actually more effective at locating them than a mine detector. That Lancaster, Pennsylvania boy saved our lives countless times. While the rest of us hid behind rocks, he laid a hand grenade beside the mines and blew them one at a time. Only the 105-round was a dud. I later recommended Jennings for a medal.

For our harbor site we chose a rock ledge on the steep mountainside giving us a good view of the valley below. I placed two men in each position and nine others about 200 feet higher up the mountain for added protection lest the enemy take position above and wipe us out. I removed my pack and sat down. As Corporal Oscar Munoz leaned back to set down his radio, he shook the bushes causing an enemy grenade to fall out . . . the vines were rigged with booby traps. As the grenade fell, the spoon flew off but it didn't explode when it hit the deck. We just looked at it, frozen with fear. Within seconds, Munoz and I sped in opposite directions, leaving packs and weapons behind. He looked back at me and said with a grin, "Hey, Lieutenant, I see there aren't any heroes in this crowd!"

Again we vacated the area, leaving Jennings to his dangerous mission. He dragged our packs and weapons to safety then laid a grenade by the enemy grenade and jumped behind the rocks before it blew. There were four other booby traps.

When we had finished eleven long-range patrols without a man being killed or wounded, my company commander, Captain Jim Schmitt, rewarded us with a day at the beach. That sounded great to me. I was glad my men could get their minds off of what they had been through in the bush. They were good troops fighting their way to the devil and back.

After company formation on Sunday, we piled into a truck and headed for China Beach. There we learned that swimming and surfing were prohibited because the monsoons were creating currents so strong that several people had drowned, including a couple of Marines. We had a football and challenged a Navy Seabees unit, an Army unit, and another Marine unit to play. I told my men, "Touch is what the girls play back home. We ought to try to impress these 'Squid'! from the Navy and 'Doggies' from the Army. They think the marines are tough . . . let's play tackle."

Clad in gym shorts and barefooted, we hit hard and played to win. We won all three games, and I felt proud as I saluted Captain Schmitt about 5:30 that afternoon.

"Lt. McClary reporting in from Red Beach, sir. Six WIA's today."

"Wait a minute!" he exploded. "You've had eleven patrols with nobody wounded. I give you a day off to go to the beach and you get six wounded. What happened? Did you get ambushed on the way back?"

"No, sir," I explained. "We played a little football. My point man, Covington, tore up his knee. We had him med-evacced out of the country. Corporal Combs broke his leg; he's in the hospital in Da Nang. Four other broke their toes." I was one of the four. I really took some ribbing for breaking my toe on my day off from fighting the war.

Losing Covington really worked on my attitude! I'd rather have lost two others than that Mississippi boy — a squirrel hunter who knew what to do in the bush. He had earlier received a purple heart. Now he would be getting a medical discharge. I went to see him before he left for further treatment. In a cast up to his waist, he laughed and teased, "Lieutenant, you-all have to go back out there in the bush and fight Charlie. I've got nothing to do but lie here in this rack!"

An assignment to Hai Van Pass in January seemed a routine mission. We were to provide surveillance against the mining and ambushing of Highway 1 from Hai Vann Pass to the south to a bridge to the north. This was the key route between Da Nang and Hue; the road was steep and crooked, cutting through the high mountain. The enemy had been hitting convoys carrying troops and supplies to the northern part of I corps. Because rain prevented our planes from flying, Charlie was giving us a fit, mining the roads at night and blowing up bridges and culverts north of the pass.

My team numbered twelve as we started to load the choppers; but Major Keating from the S-3 office stopped me, saying he needed four of my men, including my sergeant, radio man and point man. That left Corporal Munoz and six Pfc.'s to go with me. I had assigned Pfc. Johnson the "tail-end Charlie" position, leaving only "Chief" Pfc. Rod Hunter (a 19-year-old Indian from Alaska), to run point. Because he had only a little experience in that position, I felt uneasy. As we boarded the chopper Hunter quipped, "Lieutenant, don't worry. Before, it was you and the Dirty Dozen; now, it's you and the Magnificent Seven!'

Jumping out of the chopper onto some rocks in an area of low bush and vines, we slashed through trees and vines to forge our own trail. For two days we were caught in crossfire between VC snipers above us and "friendly" trucks below. Since neither the VC nor the convoys knew our exact position, enemy and friendly rounds whistled uncomfortably close.

Three days of humping had left us low on water, so I signaled that we would leave the trail to fill our canteens in a nearby stream. We were careful to put up a good defense, letting a couple of men get water while the rest covered for them. Going down to the stream, I startled two men about twelve meters from us. With weapons slung across their shoulders, they saw us as we saw them.

Hunter cut loose with his M-14, hitting one of the enemy in the lower leg. As the other went for his weapon, I shot him a couple of times and then shot the first man again. Hunter and I were about fifteen meters in front of the other six men. As we shot, a third enemy came up to our left and was about to shoot us when Corporal Munoz fired his M-16. From the stream bed another enemy fired his A-K 47, emptying 30 rounds at me and pinning me down as I tried to reach the carbine strapped to the first enemy. Bullets, shells, rocks, and branches were flying like angry hornets. As the debris struck me, I fell, more dazed than hurt. Pfc. Ford fired the M-79 killing the one in the stream and probably saving my life. I later commended Munoz and Ford for awards.

By their khakis we identified the enemy as NVA regulars. They were equipped with A-K 47s, cartridge belts and suspender straps. We were in no-man's land. We prepared to throw gas grenades, then put on gas masks and run through the haze. About this time I discovered that my nose and chin were bleeding; my foot had also been hit. Munoz signaled for Doc but I sent him back, not wanting anyone else up with me since cover was sparse.

For two days we humped through terrain so rugged that we lost radio contact with base area, which listed us missing in action. We kept moving until we could call for choppers to lift us out.

Knowing that Dea would worry more than ever, I didn't intend to tell her about my wounds; but she received a telegram anyway. There were rumors that I had been killed. The family even received some sympathy cards. I was glad it was a mistake!

When Patty and Billy heard of my wounds, Billy wrote, "Clebe, I'm so proud of you; and I know you couldn't help getting shot; but, man, if I could run the way you can, I never would have been shot in the mouth!"

I was embarrassed over all the fuss. I had almost cut myself as badly while shaving, and this hardly seemed deserving of a Purple Heart. I wrote Dea about my medal, "I don't want any more; but I hear if you get three Purple Hearts, they send you out of the country!" It would be a costly ticket home.

After being treated for superficial wounds, I took eight men to the other side of Hai Van Pass to provide surveillance against mining and ambushing of Route 1 from the pass to the south. We saw a good many woodchoppers but never knew if they actually had axes or guns. We snooped and hid without taking fire and watched, unable to help, as a large convoy heading north was ambushed. Four trucks were burned, about fifteen turned around; but a number made it through. We also saw a chopper shot down; again there was nothing we could do since it happened across the valley from us. We crossed the highest, rockiest points I'd ever attempted before reaching the South China Beach where choppers came to transport us to friendlier territory.

Von Dach with village chief and a widow. Viet Cong killed her husband.

Lt. Clebe McClary, Patrol Leader and L/Cpl Harder, Point Man on Recon Team in Vietnam (1967)

XIV

In Divine Custody

For He shall give His angels charge over thee,
to keep thee in all they ways.
Psalm 91:11 (KJV)

Recon was, by this time, covering twice the area with half as many teams as when I arrived in Vietnam, half of the men having been sent to the northern part of the country as activity there intensified.

The news reports described to troubled America an ominous scene in Southeast Asia. Immense anxiety showed in letters from home. Mom and Dad wrote in early January, "We continue to pray and worry from one letter to the next. The news on TV and radio and in the papers seems worse every day. Please use every precaution."

I don't intend to understand the anguish they suffered. Daddy kept up a strong front for the benefit of Mother, who paced the floor, pounding her hand with her fist in anger at the distant foe that she gladly would have fought for me.

Living with her family, Mr. and Mrs. Dean C. Fowler, in Florence, Dea tried to fill the lonely hours by taking nursing studies at the University of South Carolina campus in Florence and modeling at Hendrickson's, an exclusive dress shop. Spending the weekends at Friendfield, she concealed her apprehension and sought to lift the heavy hearts of Mom and Dad. Dea played my tapes for her family and mine. The recordings they made for me presented a cheerful mood to mask their sorrow and concern.

In Matthew 6:34 we are told, "Don't be so anxious about tomorrow. God will take care of your tomorrows too. Live one day at a time" (LB). That's the way I lived in Nam, one day at a time not worrying about the threat of tomorrow or even the danger at hand . . . just doing my job to the best of my ability and entrusting my safety to the Lord.

I sensed that God was leading me and my men for a special reason. When our chopper safely straddled mines that should have blown us away, I knew we were in divine custody. Family and friends bombarded Heaven with prayers for my safekeeping. More than one church had me on its prayer list.

I did what was expected of a Christian. I attended chapel services when in base area and served as battalion layman officer, filling in if a chaplain were unavailable. I recognized God's protective hand on my life and concluded that He must have some definite purpose for me, perhaps to work with youth. Preaching even occurred to me. I felt a sort of "calling," and I wondered what service He had in mind.

Time raced by. Many troops complained about how long they had been in Nam and counted the days they had left. I was so busy that I hardly noticed. I put in long hours, but I liked my work. I appreciated the discipline and the challenge of military life and thought seriously of becoming a career Marine.

I couldn't put a price tag on the experiences I had in the Corps up to that time. I'd been through a lot that I hoped I'd never see again; I expected to endure much more before leaving that battle-blemished land. All in all, it had been a sound experience and a practical education. During my year and a half in the Marines I probably learned more than in four years in college and three years of teaching and coaching. Serving in a combat zone spawns maturity . . . my daily decisions had life-or-death consequences.

"Think like a man and act like a man of thought," goes a quotation attributed to Goethe. I was a man of thought; I planned almost 24 hours a day. I tried to imagine what Charlie would do if he were me; then I did something else.

My men were well trained and cooperative. Their performance was superior and their morale was outstanding, despite the anti-war sentiment at home. Some men in my outfit had protested and demonstrated against the war while in college. When they came face to face with the Communist threat in Vietnam, they came to believe in our cause—the fight for freedom.

At this point in the war we were really trying to win. I believe this was the reason that drugs were not a problem with my men, as they proved to be later in the war when the action slowed, giving troopers more idle time. I was required to make a "pot" check periodically, walking through the enlisted men's area and sniffing to detect marijuana smoke. My troops didn't mess with that stuff, not necessarily because they were better than any other troops, but because our work involved great danger. On patrol in enemy territory, if one man coughed or stumbled and attracted Charlie, we might all be killed. My troops knew the risk. If a man played around with drugs behind my back, I suspect that his fellow troops would have cut his throat. They weren't about to jeopardize their lives for a reckless clown using "pot."

Drinking never affected the performance of my men in the bush because I permitted no drinking the day before we left on patrol. However it did concern me in base area. The beer was weaker in strength than that sold in the U. S., and the men were allowed two per day. That meant on return from the bush they were entitled to twelve or more beers. Those who didn't drink gave theirs away, making 20 to 30 beers for some men; and they seemed to think it would drown their troubles.

Between assignments we kept up our physical conditioning by lifting weights and playing football on the chopper pad, choosing sides for an hour's game. Whoever was losing at the end of that time had to run four miles to the PX and back. The losing team usually griped, but it was a good way to keep in fair shape. If I were on the winning team, I still ran with the losers to keep them going.

I didn't harass the troops about trivial details. I expected them to keep their weapons clean, know how to throw a grenade, and run with me to keep fit so that we could scramble if Charlie took after us. The men asked if I were ever on the chain gang, grumbling, "Lieutenant, you sure work us!" I told them I learned it all from my Daddy!

During my limited time at base area, I conducted drills with the men in the rice paddies, practiced rapelling, and taught classes. These covered such areas as plotting artillery and air support, radio communication, and patrol movement. The classes not only prepared the men well for patrol but also kept them from becoming slack while waiting at base area between assignment.

My men did their best . . . they prepared for the worst. After a corpsman serving with another recon team died of wounds suffered when he stepped on a mine, I had the chief corpsman and our Doc give my men a two-hour class on first-aid for bullet and mine wounds. They made all of us draw blood out of each other's veins so that we would be able to give blood in the event our corpsman were hit. It was a terrible experience but a precaution that could save lives.

Doc was a big morale factor on patrol. Nobody wanted him to get hurt. The wounded always called for the corpsman or the chaplain. Looking back, I would say a chaplain serving in the combat area should pray with every man before he gets on the helicopter and find out how he stands with the Lord. Plenty of chaplains wanted to ride the chopper and watch my men jump out, but none of them ever witnessed to me about the Lord. Perhaps they thought I was a Christian because of my high moral standards. I almost went to hell with high moral standards.

As the battle activity accelerated, a truce for the Vietnamese observance of Tet the Buddhist New Year-was like intermission in a war movie . . . time out to catch our breath. My platoon received permission to take gifts to Vietnamese families in Phuoc Ly Hoa Minh, a village of 232 in Hoa Vang District, Quang Nam Province. The village chief had me at his table for hot tea, rice bread and cookies while my men were served rice wine and tiger beer. This pleasant interlude was just the calm before the storm.

The enemy launched an offensive attack during Tet, hitting all of the major cities in South Vietnam except Da Nang. On a recon mission my unit spotted an estimated 900 enemy crossing a lake, walking four to nine abreast, carrying a variety of weapons in the direction of Da Nang. We called in air support and artillery, resulting in a number of the enemy killed. As a result our team received a Presidential unit citation commending our action. I believe it halted an offensive attack planned for Da Nang.

Assigned to Dong Den, a radio relay station which had been mortared, we filled over 1000 bags with rock and dirt to build bunkers and then set up a 50-caliber machine gun. Then we used logs to build dummy weapons, including machine guns, complete with dummy men to operate them. Helmets set on top of sand bags were to make Charlie think we had more men. In the fog and darkness, they were convincing. Apparently Charlie fell for the trick; the patrol was uneventful.

When another recon unit was pinned down by hostile fire outside of Da Nang with two men wounded, the colonel sent me to the area with 25 men and authority to do whatever I deemed best to handle the situation. We pulled out the team that had been pinned down and then ran a search-and-destroy mission through a large village, using a 13-year-old Vietnamese girl as interpreter. The VC had preceded us and shot up many homes. For protection against future attack, the villagers were digging safety tunnels and building bunkers. Our six-hour search netted no VC, though we found some traces of the enemy.

I was then assigned a mission to take five of my men, two demolition men, and Lieutenant Colonel Butler to search for a rocket site in Happy Valley where a chopper carrying another team on patrol had been shot down, killing the radio man and wounding nine others. A POW who supposedly knew where "a thousand rockets were hidden" accompanied us. When we began taking 50-and 60-caliber machine gun rounds, we suspected he was leading us into a trap and pulled back without finding the enemy rockets. Happy Valley was so labeled by the troops because they were happy to get out of there alive . . . we were happy to make it out this time.

With 18 patrols completed more than any other lieutenant in the battalion I began a mission due west of Da Nang. Our assignment was to flip-flop with "Elf Skin," a recon unit that had been hit by enemy rockets for five nights. I took 23 men to Ba Na, twelve air miles from Da Nang (forty miles by land) and nearly 5,000 feet above sea level. Once a resort area used by the French military officers, Ba Na must have been beautiful in its day; but to us it looked like a movie scene of a war-ravaged village. There were the remains of a church school and a hotel with swimming pool and tennis courts. Concrete park benches were crumbling along the trails.

Taking half a dozen men while the rest remained to defend our position, I ran some short patrols down near Happy and Leech Valley, not venturing too far because we were near Laos and too far out to receive artillery and air support. We were on alert all night because the enemy could hide in the many caves and tunnels in the area and sneak right up on us. We had a couple of skirmishes but no real battles.

Being socked in by clouds, we tired of this "easy" patrol that stretched from the planned ten day to twenty-eight days. The skies cleared long enough for choppers to drop C-rations, ammo, and mail; then clouds enveloped the hill again before we could be lifted out. I suspect the pilots were a little afraid of the risk, too, since a chopper had been shot down in the area earlier. Cold, bored, and tired of drinking rain water, we were eager to get back to normal bush patrols. The days dragged by.

As I was writing letters one night, Pfc. Johnson ran in, his eyes big as plates, exclaiming, "Great Lawd, Lieutenant! The whole blessed hill done lit up. They is everywhere! Come quick!"

I grabbed my shotgun and went running into the night expecting to find Charlie all over us. It was only a small gap in the clouds in which the lights of Da Nang were peeping through. I understood how it startled him. For 19 days, we hadn't been able to see the moon or stars, hardly whatever we had in front of our faces. Then to have lights! They did look close, but almost immediately the clouds socked us in again.

About dusk each night I went from bunker to bunker reading the men a story from Julian Bolick's The Return of the Gray Man, who according to legend heralds the approach of every storm at Pawleys Island. I had written to Mr. Bolick, who lived in Clinton, South Carolina, telling how much the men enjoyed the story. He answered saying he was sending a copy of his latest collection, Ghosts from the Coast, containing an account that came from my Grandmother McClary, "Maum Nanny and the Plateye." The tales from around home brought back fond memories for me, and my men really liked the stories the Yankee troops and Johnson most of all. One of a dozen children, Johnson had a brother serving in Vietnam with the Army. I had papers that would send him home in a few weeks.

My men spent a lot of time digging for old wine bottles that I intended to send to Dea. Johnson muttered, "Sir, you think she really gonna want these old bottles?" The troops warned me that if they got killed while hunting for bottles, they would haunt Dea!

One of my radio men was stricken with malaria and suffered with a fever of 100 to 102 for several days before we were evacuated. Two Jolly Green Giants large choppers needed in the mountainous regions for their lift power and radar equipment brought another team to flip-flop with us. When the first chopper landed and the incoming lieutenant unloaded with six men, I boarded the helicopter with six of my men. In my eagerness to get back to more important work than Ba Na seemed to be, I unintentionally violated the standing rule that the patrol leader be last to board. We lifted off as the second chopper prepared to land for the other men. At base area I had finished my shower and shave before realizing that the rest of the team had not arrived. I was told to report to the major.

Major Keating gave me the sternest reprimand that I received in Nam. He let me know that leaving men behind, even with another lieutenant, was not the way to operate. As soon as our helicopter had lifted off, clouds set in, preventing the second chopper from landing. However the clouds lifted by afternoon and the men were extracted before dark. Realizing that my haste could have endangered their lives, I knew I was wrong and deserved the rebuke; but it hurt. I highly respected Major Keating and regretted having disappointed him. A few weeks later he was killed in action.

Eager to return to the bush, I received orders assigning me to Blankenship O. P. atop Hill 452-another easy mission. Lt. Jim Barta was assigned to "Dodge City," a hot battle area in the Quan Duc Valley about thirty miles southwest of Da Nang. Since Barta had just completed a tough assignment to Charlie Ridge while my last patrol had been almost like R & R, I suggested that we swap patrols. He drew illustrations of the area since he had been there before. It would be my last patrol before meeting Deanna in Hawaii March 16 and my last bush assignment in Nam.

I had been asked to be an aerial observer, flying in a small plane to spot targets for jet bombers and call artillery from guns and Navy ships. It would have been safe work compared to jungle snooping, but I turned down the offer. I had grown close to my men and wanted to stay with them. After R & R, I expected to be promoted to company commander with three platoons under my supervision. I had delayed R & R until I could tell Dea that my bush fighting was behind me when we celebrated our first anniversary in Hawaii. While there, I was to serve as best man in the wedding of Corporal Munoz, 23-year-old Marine from Senger, California. As a wedding present I hoped to get a job for him out of the bush; Ba Na was his last patrol before R & R. I had only one to go.

The McClary Family, Grand Teton Natioal Park, Wyoming

On the Chopper Pad at An Hoa L/Cpl. Combs, Cpl. Giordano, Lt. McClary

Radioman Oscar Munos—Clebe was asked to be his best man in his wedding.

XV

The Taste of Death

Greater love hath no man than this, that a man lay down his life for his friend.
John 15:13 (KJV)

I never thought I'd be hit. It was not arrogance but rather confidence in myself, in my men, and in God who had seen us safely through danger time and time again. I had no dark premonitions about the mission to Hill 146, a stationary combat observation post deep in enemy-controlled territory. In five months as patrol leader I hadn't lost a man; I didn't expect to this time.

My 13-man team included some veteran troops: Pfc. Ralph Johnson; Pfc. Tom Jennings; Pfc. Rod Hunter; and Cpl. Bob Lucas. Most of the other men were new, including Lance Cpl. Thomas L. Jones, Pfc. H. G. "Henry" Covarrubias, Ofc. Burkhart and Navy Corpsman Shawn Green. Most of my regulars had left the bush for office assignment.

Hill 146 measured roughly 75 meters from east to west and 50 meters from north to south. As our chopper hovered in a cleared area for us to jump out, the propellers stirred up dirt that had concealed the three box mines. Pfc. Jennings hit the deck and cut the wires to the mines. My radio man and corpsman dug a foxhole to my left, and three other men took cover in a foxhole to my right; the remaining eight were at the western end about fifty yards behind me around the perimeter of a bomb crater, which was about twenty feet deep. We were in an excellent position to fight.

I felt secure yet uneasy. We guessed the enemy was up to something . . . something big. Through two tense days and nights, we watched and waited. I had a feeling we were going to get hit.

The silence of the third day warned us to get ready. We were aware of the NVA's ability to move silently through even the most rugged terrain. Usually they knew the exact shape of the position they intended to attack and where the patrol leader would be. The hill was terraced into what was almost a stairway up the sides.

Lieutenant Barta radioed from Blankenship O. P. to see how things were going. I told him that enemy rockets and mortars indicated we were in for a long night. Reminding me that we were to meet our wives in Hawaii in a few days, he cautioned, "Take care."

The darkness settled heavy with foreboding. We looked and listened.

It was just after midnight, March 3, 1968, my wife's birthday, when the attack came.

The men to my right cried out as a grenade fell into their foxhole. Johnson jumped on it, smothering it with his stomach to protect his two buddies. He died a hero and received posthumously the Medal of Honor. One of the pair, Jennings, was struck by shrapnel. The small wound apparently cut an artery causing him to bleed profusely. He lingered moments from death. Seven others, including our corpsman, Shawn Green, and our radio man were wounded in the initial assault. My whole team was about to be wiped out. We had to keep fighting. I moved from one position to another directing our defense.

By this time I had lost my left hand.

Another grenade came in. I saw it in time to throw up my right hand to protect my face. The pain! As if an axe had split my head! The left eye was torn out, the vision in my right eye blurred by blood. The blast had burst both ear drums and mutilated my right hand.

If I could reach the bomb crater . . .

But another grenade struck my legs.

Death looked me over a helpless heap of bleeding flesh and broken bones.

Suddenly there was movement behind me.

"Lieutenant! Lieutenant!"

"Chief! Is that you?" I gasped.

"Yes, sir!" It was Pfc. Hunter.

Kneeling by my feet, he began picking off the enemy as they came up the hill.

Corporal Lucas had bolted from the bomb crater to search for me when he saw the NVA ready to shoot me in the head. Lucas shot him first, causing the enemy bullet to pierce my arm. Having saved my life once, he knelt by my head and returned enemy fire.

I told Lucas to take over the patrol and call for helicopters to come in after us. He radioed the pilots; they told him that because of rain and fog, they couldn't come until daylight.

"Forget it!" he told them. "Nobody'll be left at daylight!"

We had been issued only five grenades per man, though I had requested ten. In no time they were gone. My men than threw rocks down the side of the hill, hoping the enemy would think they were grenades and retreat.

The pilots reconsidered and decided to come immediately.

Meanwhile we called in two "Spooky" units World War II cargo planes that flew at night, equipped with Vulcan guns that harnassed enough fire power to kick up dirt every square foot for 100 yards. They were reserved for whoever was getting hurt the worst. I had requested them on other occasions but never got them. They could have been on the other side of the country, but the Lord sent them to us. They were the only thing that kept up our morale.

If the NVA had followed up the initial assault, we would have been wiped out. Attacking from three sides-north, east and south they had avoided the western side where our machine gun was set up. Thus it became impossible for us to use the machine gun without shooting our own men.

Creeping silently to within 15 to 20 yards of our position without being detected, they had disconnected all our mines and booby traps. With ten of our thirteen men dead or wounded, we would have been an easy conquest if they had followed through. Perhaps the suicide squad killed more of themselves than they expected, or we killed more than they thought we would. It must have taken a while for them to reorganize at the bottom of the hill. Whatever the reason, it helped save our lives by giving us time.

Doc Green regained consciousness and began fighting to save my life. I believe that God used those many years of athletic training to keep me alive. My pulse rate was 36 beats per minute; the average is 75. Had my heart beat at a normal rate, I could have bled to death. My left arm, severed just below the elbow, did not bleed as much as it would have if amputated above the joint. The arteries appeared to have been seared off by the hot metal from the grenade. Doc put a tourniquet on the stump of my arm and started to tie off my left leg which was shredded like hamburger. Knowing that I would lose it for sure if a tourniquet were applied, I kicked him away. Because I had sustained head wounds, morphine could not be administered for pain.

The first chopper to land on the hill about 1 a.m. was loaded with the wounded, dead, and dying. The rest of the men piled into the second chopper, all except Chief Hunter and me. The chopper crew thought I was dead and urged Chief to leave me behind. He ignored their plea and risked his own life to save my life a second time.

Grabbing me under the arms, Chief dragged me 50 yards to the chopper, lifted me aboard, and held me, my legs dangling out, as the helicopter took off. Immediately some one hundred and fifty NVA stormed the hill. A delay of just minutes and not one of us would have left that hill alive.

The pain from the wounds and the cold air proved almost unbearable by the time we landed twenty minutes later at Marble Mountain Hospital near Da Nang.

Attendants hustled me onto a stretcher and began cutting away my blood-drenched clothes.

"Don't cut my boots! They'll be ruined!" I objected feebly.

They snipped them anyway as I'd seen them do to dying troopers before. Then they started cursing and slapping me.

Why did they bring me this far to beat me to death!

Aching and angry, I tried to strike back. The tactic worked . . . most of my veins had collapsed from loss of blood; but the slapping and cursing made me respond, reviving a vein in the temple.

I felt the prick of a small needle, and as the life-sustaining blood began to flow, mercifully I lost consciousness.

Jennings died half an hour after reaching the hospital. Burkhart, suffering multiple shrapnel wounds, was med-evacced out of the country. Five others were treated for minor shrapnel wounds.

For days I lingered closer to death than life. I was vaguely aware of a frantic effort to keep me alive. Tubes protruded from my torn body like hoses from a car engine. My anguish was equal to a taste of hell.

The men of my platoon paraded by, one at a time, for a last look. Lieutenant Barta cried like a baby. Marines don't cry — his eyeballs sweated! "Top" Barker refused to come. He said he wanted to remember me as I was because I was the only lieutenant he ever knew "worth a cuss."

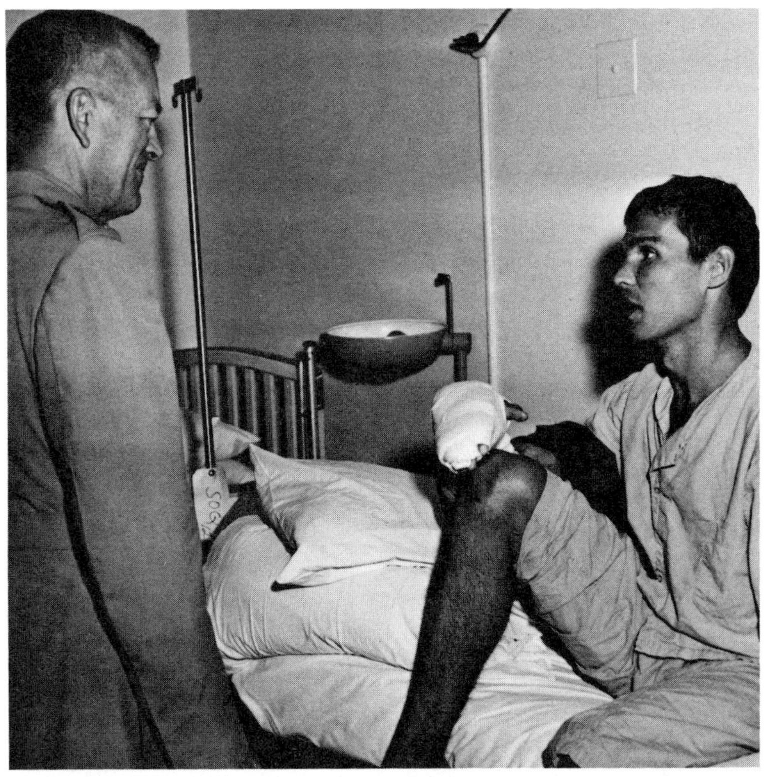

General Leonard F. Chapman, Jr., Marine Commandant visits Clebe in the hospital.

XVI

Prognosis Poor, Outlook Dim

Although the fig tree shall not blossom, neither shall fruit be in the vines; the labour of the olive shall fail, and the fields shall yield no meat; the flock shall be cut off from the fold, and there shall be no herd in the stalls. Yet I will rejoice in the Lord, I will joy in the God of my salvation. The Lord God is my strength.
Habakkuk 3:17-19 (KJV)

Deanna picks up the story:

My clothes were packed; only last-minute details remained before Mrs. McClary and I would leave to join Clebe in Hawaii.

My own Mother and I had just walked into Shirley Meyer's beauty shop when someone said, "If Deanna McClary is here, tell her she has a phone call."

"Something bad has happened to Clebe!" I cried, running to the phone.

"Come home," Aunt Estelle said guardedly. "Two men from the Marine Corps need to talk with you."

"He's dead! I know he's dead!" I sobbed to mother all the way.

Turning into the driveway, I parked behind the military truck and ran up the steps to the back porch where a Major Burleson and a doctor waited with the inevitable telegram from the commandant of the U. S. Marine Corps.

It read:

TELEGRAM

AB89 CTD226 =A

CT WA 225 XV GOVT PD = WASHINGTON DC 6 NFT =

MRS PATRICK C MC CLARY III=

DON'T PHONE 2112-A TIMMONSVILLE HWY FLORENCE SOCAR=

A REPORT RECEIVED THIS HEADQUARTERS REVEALS THAT YOUR HUSBAND SECOND LIEUTENANT PATRICK C MCCLARY III USMC SUSTAINED INJURIES ON 3 MARCH 1968 IN THE VICINITY OF QUANG NAM REPUBLIC OF VIETNAM FROM A HOSTILE GRENADE WHILE ON A PATROL. HE SUFFERED TRAUMATIC AMPUTATION OF THE LEFT ARM AND SUSTAINED SHRAPNEL WOUNDS TO ALL EXTREMITIES. PROGNOSIS POOR. OUTLOOK DIM. YOUR GREAT ANXIETY IS UNDERSTOOD AND YOU ARE ASSURED THAT HE WILL RECEIVE THE BEST OF CARE. YOU SHALL BE KEPT INFORMED OF ALL SIGNIFICANT CHANGES IN HIS CONDITION.

The major gripped me. "Mrs. McClary, he's alive!"

Alive!

I tried to absorb the word.

I sat there in unbelief as the truth soaked in. Could this tragedy actually be real, this thing that happens only to other people?

I started crying . . . but I really didn't want to cry.

Clebe's alive! That's GOOD news! But still I cried . . . I hurt for him.

All I wanted now was to find out where he was and to be with him.

Major Burleson tried several calls to Washington for a more recent report on Clebe's condition and location but was told we would be notified as soon as there was any news.

It was a sad task calling Clebe's Mother at the Georgetown County Health Department where she worked. When she answered the phone, I began crying. There was no gentle way to say it . . . Clebe lay near death on the other side of the world.

The word spread like forest fire throughout Georgetown and Florence. Among the first to come was Mrs. Givens (Florence) Young, sister-in-law of Congressman Ed Young. She contacted Major Julian Dusenbury, a World War II hero, paralyzed from the waist down, who was active in politics. He began calling Congressmen and Senators. Senator Strom Thurmond and Congressman John McMillan learned that Clebe would be med-evacced to Japan.

Clebe:

I arrived in Japan in the custody of a couple of Army medics who for some reason couldn't find the right hospital. It was cold and snowing-a drastic change from the muggy weather of Vietnam-and I was groaning with pain. One of the medics growled, "Stick a cigarette in his mouth and he'll shut up!"

I have never smoked in my life. I gagged and spat it out, thinking a slap would have hurt less.

After being misdirected to three hospitals we arrived at the U. S. Army 249th General Hospital at Camp Drake, Japan. Here I engaged in my toughest skirmish of the war-the battle for my life.

Despite heavy sedation, I bordered on delirium. I thought I was talking to Dea but couldn't be sure. She telephoned twice, but I couldn't hear her. The grenade had burst both ear drums and caused drainage so that my hearing was terribly distorted.

Few areas of my body had escaped injury. Surgery was followed by more surgery. More than anything I wanted to go home. I knew I could recover if I could just see Dea again. As plans were being made to med-evac me to the U. S., my temperature soared. Then came chills and a recurrence of fever. Malaria was suspected, but blood smears failed to confirm it.

As great as the physical pain was, my mental anguish was greater over the ruin of the plans Dea and I had for Hawaii; but that was the least of her worries.

Deanna:

A second telegram from the Pentagon indicated that Clebe's condition had become more stable but remained serious. I felt as if I were not actually living through this nightmare. I couldn't visualize Clebe with only one arm. Just two weeks earlier he had sent a photo showing his two strong arms bronzed by the tropical sun.

At night sleep came slowly. Was it days or merely hours that had passed? A shrill ring broke the silent night. The phone! Oh, dear God! I was afraid to answer . . . afraid of what the news might be.

Clebe's father choked as he spoke. "Dea, honey, a friend of ours just called from Japan. Clebe has been flown there. He's in bad shape. One eye has been blown out!"

Oh, no! no!

That rugged, handsome face ripped to shreds!

This news struck a deeper blow than the report of the loss of his arm. Clebe's almond eyes had been the windows of his life to me. He seemed to look through me and know my every thought.

An eye blown out! What must it look like? A dark, empty space? Hurry, morning! I hated the night. I couldn't live with my thoughts of the unknown.

Desperately I clung to one thought . . . he's alive! Somehow nothing else mattered. Clebe was special to me because of his love, his character, his inner strength. Losing an arm or an eye wouldn't change that.

God had so blessed our love that we truly became as one. Away from him, I seemed only half a person.

I must go to him . . . help him fight to live!

Another telegram prepared me for the amputation of his left leg.

Dear God, Please, Please let him live until we can be together! Oh, time, how much longer must I wait?

Clebe:

The Defense Department encouraged Dea to wait, saying I might be returned to the States any day; but to me it seemed forever!

My family (as I learned later) suffered greatly during those days of uncertainty. A multitude of friends came to Friendfield or called high school and college pals of mine, Pawleys Island and Georgetown friends, old and young, black and white. Cards, letters and telegrams poured in to the plantation from across the country. Practically every coach I knew sent a remembrance. Captain Mack and Miss Teeny took a seafood dinner to my parents. My old room buddy, Tommy Liles, drove to Georgetown to visit Mom and Dad and went on to Florence to see Dea.

The first thing Daddy did was to shop for a light gun that I could use for hunting. It was an attempt to conceal his emotions and to strengthen his hope for my recovery. My father remembered me as "the finest specimen of manhood" he had ever seen. Now he knew not what to expect.

Colonel Seth Dingle, a family friend, had come to visit me immediately after I arrived in Japan. He then telephoned my parents to report on my condition, telling them for the first time about the loss of the eye. I still didn't know.

My appearance was such that Colonel Dingle wouldn't allow his wife to visit me for several days.

Tape covered my left eye; my face was full of stitches. Many teeth were badly broken. The stump of my left arm was bandaged. My right arm was in a cast. The fingers were stiff and sore, the nails having been ripped off by the grenade blast. My right leg was full of shrapnel, the left one shredded.

The Dingles visited regularly, bringing fresh strawberries, fruits and juices, cookies, magazines and cheerful conversation about home and people we knew.

Colonel Dingle examined my feet and summoned a nurse, asking her to "do something" about them. They were black and it looked as if gangrene had set in. I explained that I didn't wear socks in Nam because they were slow to dry in the tropical climate and could cause jungle rot. He responded, "Socks! You must not have worn any shoes with feet like those!"

Dr. Hunter Stokes, an ophthalmologist from Florence, and his wife, Patsy (a friend of Patty's at Winthrop College), were also in Japan with the Army. They were stationed about fifty miles from the hospital and traveled by helicopter to visit me frequently. Dr. Stokes removed some stitches from my face and broke the shocking news to me — the left eye was gone.

I hadn't even considered the possibility! That night on Hill 146, I couldn't see but thought it was only the blood in my eyes! Even the patch hadn't made me suspect that the eye was torn out. I thought it was damaged but not beyond repair. Strangely, I was overcome not with grief at the news. Rather, I felt gratitude that my mangled right hand, now hanging limp and useless had protected my right eye and saved me from a life of blindness.

In the bed next to mine was Corporal Stuart Simmons of Florence, South Carolina. He had graduated from high school with Dea. I viewed it as nothing less than a miracle that we met in the hospital ward in Japan. Stuart lost a leg in combat at Hue, yet he concealed his own suffering to help me. He poured water and held the glass for me to drink and wrote Dea the letters that I dictated.

In the pre-op ward, being prepared for yet another surgery, I heard a familiar voice.

"McClary! What in the world are you doing here?"

It was Steve Munson, a Marine who had been a close friend at Quantico. We hadn't seen each other since training. Steve sustained a back injury in Nam, but he could walk. Ignoring his own pain, he took me to a movie one night, pushing me in a wheelchair down cobblestone streets. I couldn't see or hear well enough to enjoy the movie, but his kindness meant a great deal to me.

After a bout with gangrene, my left leg was saved, and the healing process began. When I grew strong enough to take a few steps the men in the ward cheered. It would be a long road back to anything close to a normal life.

A black soldier who had lost a leg offered to take care of me. The food we were served was greasy and cold. Since my teeth were broken, I was given hominy soup or something else so tasteless that I couldn't eat it. My friend tried to feed me, insisting, "This is good, Lieutenant. You ought to eat it." We took turns. He ate a bite then stuck the same spoon in my mouth!

I wrote home daily, relying on the Red Cross and USO workers, Stuart, or other patients to pen my thoughts. I now felt strong enough to overcome my handicap; what I worried most about was the suffering Deanna endured.

"Please don't let this get you down," I pleaded in a letter dated March 16, 1968. "I will recover before long, and we can fulfill our dreams and never be apart again. I'm sorry I had to ruin this first anniversary. If things had gone as we had planned, we would be in Hawaii today."

I thanked God for what I still had. It seemed that most of the men who had lost legs were happy to have arms because they liked to work with their hands. I lost an arm but was glad to keep my legs because running had been my interest. I pitied some patients who lay hoping for a leg transplant.

All I wanted was to go home. When Colonel H. P. Williamson presented me the Bronze Star with Combat V and a citation, I offered to swap them for a ticket home.

Part of the citation follows: "During the afternoon of 3 March, 1968, he was commanding a thirteen-man patrol deep in the enemy controlled Quan Duc Valley, when his unit was attacked by a numerically superior enemy force utilizing mortars, automatic weapons, and hand grenades. During the initial attack, he was seriously wounded in the arms, legs and face by fragments of an exploding hand grenade, resulting in the loss of his left arm below the elbow. Resolutely disregarding his painful injuries, he continued to move from one position to another, encouraging his men and directing their fire until he fell to the ground unconscious, due to the severity of his wounds. Throughout, his bold initiative and aggressiveness were an inspiration to all who observed him. Second Lieutenant McClary's extreme courage, exceptional leadership, and devotion to duty throughout were in keeping with the highest traditions of the Marine Corps and of the United States Naval Service."

I felt some pride in this recognition, but I needed more than pride.

XVII

Why Me, Lord?

And we know that all things work together for good to them that love God, to them who are called according to His purpose.
Roman 8:28 (KJV)

I knew enough about God not to question His ways. I could not imagine what purpose He had in my experience, but I tried to sound convincing as I encouraged Dea on a tape, "The Bible teaches that everything happens for the best for those who love the Lord. I look at my arm, and I think about my eye; and I wonder . . . but I guess you shouldn't question the Bible. At least I'm living."

The time did come when I asked, "Why me, Lord?"

Taking a good look at myself and remembering how beautiful Deanna was, I began to think she would be better off without me. I became so depressed that I gave up. I lost my desire to live.

Dea had just won the beauty contest in the wards of our hospital. Each patient entered a picture of his wife or girlfriend. Names were omitted, and the "contestants" were numbered; patients in the other ward voted on pictures from my ward and vice versa. Dea was selected the most beautiful girl and honored with a crudely designed certificate reading "Miss 884 awarded to Dea McClary by the men of the 249th General Hospital Osaka, Japan." I was very proud of her.

People had teased me by asking good-naturedly what a beautiful girl like Dea was doing with somebody like me. I quipped. "It's my personality and Southern charm!", but suddenly it wasn't funny any more. I wondered, too, and wished I could die.

I was discouraged by the anti-American sentiment expressed by demonstrators who threw rocks through hospital windows. Just when I needed help the most, God used professional golfer Billy Casper to pick me up. At the time I didn't care much about golf or know much about Casper, who was on a visit to the wards.

Someone told him, "That fella's in pretty bad shape. Just go on to the next bed." Casper stopped anyway, laid down a small picture, and said a few words to me. I don't remember what he said, but it made me think that somebody cared. Here was a man on a tour, visiting a hospital where people were shot up. He came because he cared. In a way, God probably used him to save my life. His concern gave me the lift I needed on the difficult road to recovery.

I thank God for Billy Casper and other athletes, beauty queens, actors and actresses who go to veterans' hospitals and children's homes. It's not an easy assignment, but I know what it means to the patients because I've been one.

Billy Casper went on to win the Masters Golf Tournament in 1968. I saw him at the Masters competition later, with my arm still in a cast. I told him what he had meant to me. I'll always be grateful to him for helping to restore my desire to live.

Letters of encouragement boosted my spirits. A note from some of the men in Texas Pete said, "We hope you're feeling better, and we will all miss having you around here. We'll always consider you a great leader and the best one ALPHA Company ever had." It was signed by Corporal R. D. Lucas, Private First Class R. J. Bury, Jr., Private First Class R. A. Hunter, Private First Class H. G. "Henry" Covarrubias, Private First Class R. A. Batemen,

Private First Class S. W. MacDonald, Corporal Oscar Munoz, Lance Corporal Thomas L. Jones, and Lieutenant E. G. Meiners.

In a letter several months later, Covarrubias identified himself as "the new guy who went on my first patrol to Hill 146." He added, "When you were here, I learned a lot from you; and I will never forget you as a friend and great leader. Maybe that is why I'm still alive."

Bury, who made five patrols with me, later wrote, "Lieutenant McClary taught me many things that I found very vital later in my tour. The thing that the Lieutenant did best, I thought, was reading a map. He always knew where we were within 200 meters. I had a lot of respect for Lieutenant McClary, not just as an officer, but mainly as a man. The Lieutenant pushed teamwork in and out of the field. He wanted the team cross-trained in every job in the team, for one day or night it might mean our life. He also not only treated his men as men and as individuals, but listened to their opinions. I not only had respect for the Lieutenant, but I had enough confidence in him to follow him to Hanoi."

Corporal Tom Hyder of Arizona wrote, "I have met many inspiring men. To me you were among the greatest. Your active zeal, your continual smile, and sincere interest in your fellowmen was a testimony to us all. May God be with you always."

Colonel B. C. Stinemetz, who was on R & R when I was wounded, wrote a few days after his return, "I was quite depressed to learn of the wounds you received, but I'm bolstered by the fact that I know of no other officer in this battalion who by virtue of character could have weathered them as well as you. The battalion, Company A, and particularly 'Texas Pete' will miss you, both personally and professionally. No officer in this battalion has ever demonstrated more leadership qualities and moral character demanded of a Marine Corps officer than you. Permit me to extend my most sincere 'thank you' for the enormous contribution you made to this battalion and to the Marine Corps. There is no question in my mind that if the same dedication and enthusiasm you exhibited in this battalion accompany you wherever you go, you will succeed."

The letters were also a source of strength and comfort to Dea. Lieutenant Jim Barta, who was originally assigned the patrol that almost cost me my life, said, "He was and still is the most respected and best liked officer in this battalion. This feeling runs from private to lieutenant colonel without exception. Dea, to this day, I wish that it had been I, not Clebe, who was hit. He was too good and too fine a man to suffer. I owe him a lifetime debt."

Major Daniel J. Keating, Jr., was killed in action shortly after writing, "Pat was held in high regard by all officers and men of his battalion. He impressed me as a dedicated and professional leader whose only concern was the accomplishment of his mission and the welfare of the men under his command. You can be assured that your husband by his actions set the finest example possible both in the camp and in the field. His loss to the battalion cannot be measured; and if it is some small consolation, Pat in the future will continue to have the same effect on the youth of America."

Captain Jim Schmitt, my first company commander who later worked with the Republic of Korea (ROK) Marines in Vietnam, said in a recent letter, "Clebe joined Company A. Recon Battalion, First Marine Division straight from Basic School. He was and still is a very sincere, dedicated officer. He was the best of all my platoon commanders and displayed excellent leadership. He was able to command his men's respect as well as their admiration while leading them on patrols. He was aggressive and tried to really go after the NVA. He was an excellent Marine officer. I think that Clebe may have come back from the 'edge of darkness' after he was wounded to bring 'light and hope' to many people in our land who are 'lost.' He will be able to help many people by bringing Christ's message to them."

First Lieutenant Eugene G. Meiners, my company commander after Captain Schmitt, wrote to Dea, "Permit me to say that your husband is one of the finest young men I have ever known. The men of Texas Pete and Chili Pepper looked upon him with an admiration and respect that is uncommon even in Marines. His fellow officers hold him in the highest regard of any of his contemporaries. As for myself, I find it hard to put it in words. Pat has some certain inner quality that sets him apart from other men yet tends to draw others to him."

Chaplain David J. Williams said, "Pat left a crystal clear resounding testimony in the entire battalion here. With Christ ruling and reigning we know that the disappointment and heartache of 3 March will be turned to praise and thanksgiving."

South Carolina Governor Robert E. McNair wrote to me, "All of us in South Carolina want you to know that we are thinking of you and wishing there were something we could do to express our deep gratitude for all you have done for your country. This is impossible but perhaps knowing you are uppermost in our thoughts will make these dark days a little brighter."

Claymon Grimes, state Senator from Georgetown and a close family friend, wrote, "I received the distressing news concerning your injuries yesterday. Needless to say we were all terribly upset but I can only say 'thank God you're alive.' We are all praying for your speedy recovery."

Coach Bill Dufford wrote, "I have seen other days when ole Clebe had the cards pretty well stacked against him and he came through with flying colors. I'm sure this will be the case now. They really can't keep a good man down."

When it appeared that I might have to stay in Japan for several more months, Daddy called Senator Strom

Thurmond to see if he could obtain clearance for Dea to come to Japan. But by the end of March arrangements were made to transfer me to Bethesda Naval Hospital in Maryland. Dea stayed with my parents, waiting to hear when I would arrive.

When Senator Thurmond's office called about 3 p.m. saying I would be at Bethesda that night, they reserved the last three seats on a 5 p.m. flight from Charleston to Washington. About midnight they were notified that I was at the hospital and were asked to wait until morning to visit because the trip had been tiring for me.

Deanna:

The elevator doors opened onto an immaculate corridor which immediately filled with uniformed personnel. Doctors and nurses surrounded us and tried to prepare us for the shock of seeing Clebe. They warned us that he would be sensitive to our reaction to his appearance. Instantly, I heard his voice echoing down the hall. It sounded muffled but there was no mistaking it.

"Which room is my husband in?" I asked anxiously. "I've waited too long now. I don't really care what he looks like . . . I just want to be by his side. Please talk to his Mother and Dad, but I must go. I can't wait another minute."

They pointed out a room to the left at the end of the corridor.

I walked briskly, trying to control my pounding heart. Magnetized by the voice, I stopped before the open door and peeked in. Thinking I had the wrong room, I turned to leave, shocked at the sight of the two bandaged men.

"Dea, honey, it's me. Baby, I know I'm not a pretty sight, but I'm happy to be alive and home."

Clebe!, a pathetic 115 pounds, with bandages covering the left eye and both ears, head shaved, face full of stitches, stump of the left arm bound, right arm in a cast and motionless, left leg open and draining with the bone exposed, and the right leg covered with shrapnel wounds.

"You're beautiful!" I cried, running to him, wrapping my arms around his frail form gently, afraid of hurting him.

"Don't worry," I assured him. "We're going to make the best of everything."

Clebe:

She was the same wonderful Dea, acting as if nothing were different. I never really doubted that she could adjust. It didn't seem to phase her; all that mattered was our being together.

As Mother and Daddy joined us, I could only guess their emotions. It was an unusual reunion joy mingled with sadness.

Dea stayed with my mother's sister and her husband, Lucille and Dorsey Delavigne, while I was at Bethesda. Daily she came to the hospital about five o'clock in the morning and sat by my bed waiting for me to awake. She fed and bathed me, changed my bandages, and massaged my numb hand to help restore partial usefulness. The Lord surely prepared Dea for this trauma. At the time of my injuries, her nursing studies dealt with prosthetics and amputation. It hardly seemed a coincidence. Having also studied foot drops, she noticed that my feet hung forward and suggested to the doctor that it might be foot drops. He agreed and ordered a footboard right away. Because of my extended hospitalization, Dea never completed her nursing studies; but she received enough practical experience to merit a degree!

At first Dea helped by doing things for me that I couldn't do for myself. Then she helped by the opposite treatment refusing to do them. Wrapping my twisted fingers around a fork, she encouraged me to feed myself. On one of my first leaves from the hospital, she got in the car and left me standing in the rain.

"I'm not going to open doors for you for the rest of your life," she declared. "You can do it!"

I did, from that day on. Her treatment was good for me. She realized that I was not the type to be dependent on others.

The physical therapist at Bethesda, John Hetrick, literally set me on my feet. He worked with me three or four times a day, prescribing exercise to build my strength and encouragement to build my confidence.

Several operations were performed to remove metal from my head, gums, forearm, legs, and feet. One ear drum was reconstructed, using the lining of a vein in my temple. The other ear drum was rebuilt in later surgery at Philadelphia Naval Hospital. After the reconstructive surgery my hearing greatly improved. Most of my teeth had to be capped. Surgery was also performed on my left eye to remove the damaged tissue. I received an artificial eye which the eye doctor painted daily because the color of my pajamas affected the color of my right eye, and the artificial eye never seemed to match! I used the eye for about four years but found it uncomfortable to wear. Looking at it seemed to make others uncomfortable, too. I finally abandoned the eye in favor of a black patch, which doesn't appear to bother anyone.

XVIII

Rebuilding a Devastated Life

I am come that they might have life,
and that they might have it more abundantly.
John 10:10b (KJV)

When the smoke of battle clears, and the bodies are buried, and the peace is signed, then the rebuild ing starts. For me the war was over. The challenge facing me was to rebuild a devastated life.

During my first leave from the hospital in Florence, South Carolina, (Dea's hometown), an evangelistic crusade was being held at the football stadium where I had thrown and caught many touchdown passes and coached many teams. It was sponsored by the Fellowship (of Florida) Christian Athletes. I read in the newspaper that Bobby Richardson, former second baseman with the New York Yankees, and Vonda Kay Van Dyke, former Miss America from Arizona, were to participate. While coaching in Florence I had once invited Bobby to speak at my school. I said to Deanna, "I'd sure like to see Bobby Richardson," and of course, any Marine would like to see Miss America! So we went to the stadium on the night of July 26, 1968.

We heard Bobby and Vonda Kay give brief testimonies, sharing what the Lord Jesus Christ had done in their lives. Then came a message that God used to change my life. It was presented by Evangelist Billy Zeoli, president of Gospel Films, Muskegon, Michigan. His father, Anthony

Zeoli, accepted Christ in prison and had become a powerful evangelist. He was called the "walking Bible" for his knowledge of the Scriptures. Billy preached to us about some of the great men of the Bible who had become "fools for God." He spoke of Noah, who likely was labeled a fool by the people in his community when he built an ark at God's command. He told of Joshua, who must have been ridiculed by his soldiers when he announced God's battle plans for Jericho. He mentioned others who obeyed God, though it seemed foolish to men. He said that if they were fools, they were fools for God. He said there are two kinds of fools in this world — fools for Christ and fools for others. The greatest fool of all, he added, is one who hears God's plan of salvation and rejects it.

"Whose fool are you?" he asked. "Whose fool are you?"

His question seemed to slap me in the face. I realized whose fool I'd been all of my life. I never drank or smoked in order to become a good athlete and to impress people. I was a good person, playing the role people expected of me. I grew up in church and believed in the right things-the Bible, tithing, good morals, and clean habits — but I had never invited Jesus Christ into my heart as Savior or let Him become the Lord of my life.

When the invitation was given I stood. To my left Dea also stood. With my left eye gone and hearing poor in the left ear, I was not aware that God had touched us both until we walked forward together to receive Christ as personal Savior. We had difficulty finding someone to counsel with us; everyone thought we were Christians who had come to assist with the counseling! Finally the Reverend Sam Anderson, a Presbyterian minister from Hemingway, South Carolina, led us to the Lord.

Deanna's popularity and her beauty titles did not disclose the problem she struggled with, the inner emptiness that remained unsatisfied. Her parents, I knew, had given her many luxuries piano, voice, modeling and modern dance lessons, stylish clothes, practically anything money could buy; but her homelife was a nightmare. Her father owned a medical complex housing doctors' offices and a pharmacy. Driven by ambition for wealth and social prestige, he began "popping" pills and drinking heavily. Dea feared and hated him. Her inner loneliness and confusion ended when Jesus Christ came into her heart, replacing hatred with love that eventually led her father to accept Christ into his own life. Through Dea's witness, her mother also found Jesus.

My heart was changed that midsummer night, but my life did not change noticeably. For years I had tried to live the Christian life; the difference was that now Christ was living in me. When this Marine surrendered to the Lord, it was not defeat but rather victory. In the Marine Corps I had sought only to serve my country. At last, I joined the greatest Army that has ever marched the Army of Jesus Christ.

God's purpose became clear: He spared my life that I might find abundant life in Him. I did not know it at the time, but through my experiences He was to touch countless lives.

The crusade leaders asked me to give my testimony publicly the night following our commitment. I don't remember what I shared because I didn't know how to describe what had happened. New Life! Abundant and everlasting! A child of God! I couldn't explain it, but I knew it was real. It was the beginning of a ministry that was to take me across the United States numerous times as well as abroad, sharing the miracles God had performed in my life.

Immediately ahead lay the road to rehabilitation, and it was long and dreary. By spending most of my thirty-day leave on the beach, I found I would not need plastic surgery as the sun miraculously healed my facial scars. The natural foods we ate as children on the plantation, the health diet I followed as an athlete, and the years I devoted to physical conditioning all contributed, I believe, to the rapid healing of my body.

Later in the summer I was transferred to Philadelphia Naval Hospital. Dea was invited to stay at Mr. Cheston's 60-acre estate at Gwynedd Valley, Pennsylvania, about twenty-five miles from Philadelphia. Mr. Cheston had died shortly before my last patrol.

I spent the weekends with Dea at the estate; and the setting itself provided therapy beautiful lawns, acres of pheasant populated woods where I could walk with a yellow Labrador retriever. We even had a cook and maid serving us. Unaccustomed to such luxury, I was a bit embarrassed at dinner one evening. Tasting a bowl of what I thought to be soup, I concluded that it must be the most flavorless dish I had ever eaten. Dea explained that it wasn't soup at all but a finger bowl of water!

When I had to go back to the hospital for surgery, Dea stayed in Philadelphia with friends. For the winter, we found an apartment in Barrington, New Jersey, just a 20-minute drive from the hospital.

We began attending a church down the street from our apartment, Faith Presbyterian. The pastor's wife, Donna Smitley, helped me get a job at Oaklyn Junior High School where she taught English. For seven months while I underwent treatment at the hospital as an outpatient, I taught physical education at Oaklyn. I organized a track team, coached the boys' and girls' basketball teams and initiated intramural Olympic games. The students dedicated their yearbook to me and presented me with a plaque which said, "a great coach, a great teacher, but most of all, a great friend." They didn't know that they did more for me than I did for them. They helped to restore my confidence in myself.

While playing soccer with the students I fell and split the end of the bone in the stump of my left arm so that two inches had to be removed. Another two inches had been taken earlier because infection kept the wound from healing. This must have been a blessing in disguise, for I used that arm better afterwards.

My right arm was withered from being in a cast, and the fingers were drawn and useless. A clump of scar tissue in the palm was removed to release the tendons and nerves. Surgery was performed on each finger to restore as much function as possible.

Doctors had been pessimistic about my having any use of the hand. The middle finger appeared dead, but Dr. S. C. (Sig) Sandzen insisted that it could be improved. In an unusual operation he transplanted a tendon from my leg to the hand. The operation lasted longer than anticipated, and I apparently was anesthetized too long. When I could not be roused, the doctors sent Dea into the recovery room to see if she could wake me. Wearing a white robe and mask, she sat by the bed repeating, "Clebe, wake up. You're going to be all right." Suddenly I gave a start and began trembling. Seeing her dressed in white, I thought she was an angel and that I had died and gone to Heaven!

Perhaps the surgery would have been successful if I had followed Dr. Sandzen's advice. He did not favor my accepting a speaking engagement in the Minneapolis-St. Paul area. I went with Bobby Richardson, the idol of my youth whose testimony spoke to my heart at the crusade where I found Christ. There was something unusual about Bobby; I discovered that it was Jesus in him. I didn't want to miss this engagement with him.

We stayed at an athletic club where the sauna apparently affected my hand. A severe infection set in, causing the transplanted tendon to fail to function. When Dr. Sandzen called several doctors in for consultation, I thought about hunting season at Friendfield and quipped, "That's my trigger finger. If you can get it to work, forget the rest!"

To pass the hours when I was in surgery, Deanna visited some of the other young men in the Naval Hospital, many of them double and triple amputees.

Appreciative of her homemade cookies as well as her Southern charm and cheerfulness, they called her "Sunshine."

I thank God for Deanna. At the Naval Hospital I saw more than six hundred Marines and sailors return from Vietnam with arms off, legs gone, and eyes out. Over sixty percent of their wives turned their backs and walked out on their husbands. Dea has been with me every step of the way through 30 operations. Proverbs 19:14 says, "A father can give his sons houses and riches, but only the Lord can give them understanding wives." The Lord really gave me an understanding and faithful wife in Deanna.

In the room adjacent to mine at the Naval Hospital was Lieutenant Lou Puller, son of General "Chesty" Puller, probably the most decorated Marine of all time. On learning that General Puller was to visit the hospital, I decided I wanted to be shaved before meeting him. From my bed I yelled for a corpsman.

"What are you hollering about?" asked a uniformed officer from the doorway. It was General Puller himself!

"I wanted a corpsman to shave me before meeting you, sir," I explained.

"Why, Marine," he replied, "I can shave you." He then sat down on my bed and shaved me. What an introduction to a dignitary! After that meeting I talked with him many times when he came to visit his son.

A soldier patient at the hospital was trying to maneuver his wheel chair up a ramp to his room one day. The incline was rather steep and difficult to climb. When someone began pushing his wheel chair, the soldier looked around and recognized General Puller, who pushed him to the door of his ward and stopped.

"Would you mind pushing me on inside?" he asked, explaining, "Nobody in there would believe that "Chesty" Puller pushed me up the ramp!"

An Alabamian, Bobby Masters, and I were chosen as guinea pigs to test an electronic arm developed by Ford

Philco. Masters had lost both arms in Vietnam serving with the Marines. The experiment at Temple University was funded by the government. Impulses from different muscles stimulated electronic controls glued to our bodies to operate the arm. We had to think about what we were doing. If I thought, "Grab the water glass," the hook grabbed the glass and started bringing it toward me. If I thought about drinking before it actually reached my lips, the impulses responded, dumping the water in my lap. I was a little afraid of the contraption!

I was fitted with an artificial arm with hook and taught to use it. We underwent a variety of tests, such as locking and unlocking locks, pulling out chairs for someone to sit down, helping another person to put on a coat, tying a tie and shoes, cutting our fingernails, cutting meat and setting the table. I learned to use the mechanical arm efficiently, knowing that I would depend on it a great deal. However, I regained some us of my right hand and now wear the artificial arm only when I am engaged in heavy work around the house or office. The extra-strong cables I added make the arm too heavy and difficult to operate for normal use. I try to keep an extra arm in good repair for Sunday wear!

At Saturday morning "stump check," I met Gunnery Sergeant Arnold "Bud" Pate, who had invested 16 years in the Marines before arriving in Vietnam. During four months at Khe San he and 75 percent of his men were wounded. Sixteen were killed by an enemy artillery round about midnight April 18, 1968. On May 12 (Mother's Day), as "Gunny" crossed a bridge, the enemy detonated a mine, shattering his right arm which had to amputated in Okinawa. Several months later, having long felt the Lord's nudging, he surrendered to preach and now pastors a church in East Tennessee.

When I shared my testimony in a Knoxville, Tennessee, crusade in 1971, "Gunny" was called to the platform. It was an emotional meeting a handshake with our hooks for two Christian Marines in the battle for souls.

Clebe with Jim Braddock, Special Olympics, Columbia, South Carolina, May 14, 1987. Clebe and Jim, Recon and Airbourne Vets were both wounded in Vietnam, now both are running for Youth. Clebe is State Chairman of 1987 and 1988 S.C. Special Olympics.

XIX

A More Excellent Way

And yet show I unto you a more excellent way.
I Corinthians 12:31b (KJV)

All my plans for a military career were blown up on Hill 146 on the night of March 3, 1968. I received a discharge from the Marine Corps in July, 1969, and accepted a position as probation and parole officer with the State of South Carolina.

Over two hundred persons of all ages reported to me monthly, their offenses ranging from driving under the influence of an intoxicant to murder. I was able to help a number of them to find jobs so that they could support their families. One boy was diverted from a jail career and enabled to secure a college scholarship. He graduated with honors and became a fine citizen, but his case was exceptional. Many of the offenders committed other violations within a few months.

Some were roughnecks, and more than once I was called to the scene of a fight to find one participant angrily brandishing a knife or gun. One night someone shot the transformer at our house, putting out the lights while Dea was home alone. Sometimes she received calls from men using obscenity and panting over the phone. When she began reading Scriptures to them, they hung up fast. I've shared this experience across the country, and many have written saying they have tried it and found it to be a successful method of dealing with obscene calls.

Convinced that I could better serve the Lord if people came to me because they wanted to come, rather than because they had to, I resigned after eighteen months in this field. Dea and I opened a coffee house in the basement of the old Post Office building in Georgetown. We called it "The Way" because our purpose was to show young people the way to the Lord Jesus Christ, who is the only solution to their problems. In an informal setting we offered recreation, Bible study, gospel films, singing, weight lighting, "rap" sessions, private counseling and special speakers. Several volunteers assisted us.

Being in the Myrtle Beach Grand Strand area, which has a population of about 20,000 in winter and 200,000 in summer, we found it a "field white unto harvest." In 26 months we counseled some 6,000 people, youth as well as adults. We came into contact with a cross-section of humanity drug addicts, soldiers absent without leave from service, sailors who had jumped ship, girls considering abortion, alcoholics, runaways, shoplifters, other criminal offenders, people with school or marriage problems, even hired killers dealing in drugs.

Through this ministry we helped many mixed-up people to find jobs and encouraged them to turn to Jesus Christ to straighten out their lives.

Eventually I began to receive many opportunities to share my testimony; and we realized that more people could be touched with the message of Christ through a wider ministry than the limited outreach of "The Way", so we closed the coffee house. For a time I served as part-time aide to Congressman Ed Young, counseling youth and speaking in high schools.

The Reverend Sam Anderson, who organized an evangelistic outreach called Teen Crusade (modeled after the meeting we had attended in Florence) invited me to share my testimony at his meetings which were carrying the gospel to youth across America.

Through Teen Crusade Dea and I became friends with Lee and Betty Fisher. Betty was helping in the follow-up program for Teen Crusade. Lee was an associate with the Billy Graham team.

In Kannapolis, North Carolina, Dea and I were riding with Lee and Betty back to our motel after the opening service of a Teen Crusade. A police cruiser, trying to stop another auto, hit the Fisher car broadside. Dea, seven months pregnant, sustained a broken hip and began having labor pains. It was feared that she might lose our first baby. Alcohol administered intravenously halted the labor, but the doctors warned us that the baby might not be normal and that Dea likely would be unable to walk without limping. She was confined to a wheel chair for months and used crutches for a period afterwards, but Dea today has no trace of a limp. Tara was born October 22, 1969, better than normal extraordinary, in our opinion! She accepted the Lord at age five and prays for others, including her sister, Christa, born April 5, 1971.

In October, 1969, I was invited to the Billy Graham Crusade in Anaheim, California, to share with 56,000 people in Angel Stadium what God had done in my life. The service was later shown on a nationwide telecast and my testimony was carried in the April, 1970, issue of "Decision" Magazine.

The crusade appearance was one of the highlights of my life. Since Dea was still recuperating from the accident, Daddy went with me and enjoyed the experience as much as I. It was an honor to meet Dr. Graham and his team. Cliff Barrows, whose home is in Greenville, South Carolina, later invited me to speak at Wade Hampton High School in Greenville where his daughter was a student.

As invitations to speak poured in from across the country, I felt the Lord leading into full-time evangelism. After much prayer Dea and I organized the Clebe McClary Evangelistic Association in September, 1973. We asked four outstanding Christians to serve with us on the board of directors. All of them had assisted greatly in our spiritual growth: Bobby Richardson, Billy Zeoli, E. J. Daniels, and Jerry Falwell.

This unusual ministry as a layman has taken me throughout America, to every state and most of them more than once, including Alaska and Hawaii. We have witnessed in churches, evangelistic crusades, civic organizations, prisons, and over 500 high schools. I have been invited to speak to numerous groups, including the Fellowship of Christian Athletes, Campus Crusade, Youth for Christ and Word of Life, as well as in many churches.

It has been a blessing to work with dedicated pastors throughout the country, including Dr. Jerry Falwell, Dr. W. A. Criswell, Dr. Tim LaHaye, Dr. Jack Hyles, Dr. Adrian Rogers and Dr. Bob Gray. I have appeared with many evangelists, among them Dr. E. J. Daniels, James Robison, Bill Glass, Moody Adams, B. R. Lakin and Charles "Toonie" Cash.

Professional athletes have had me visit and share with them, including the Atlanta Braves, Cincinnati Reds, Houston Astros, San Diego Padres, San Francisco Giants, Los Angeles Dodgers, Cleveland Indians, New York Yankees, Milwaukee Brewers, Baltimore Orioles, Toronto Blue Jays, Detroit Tigers, Boston Red Sox and New York Mets.

Also, Chicago Cubs, St. Louis Cardinals, Philadelphia Phillies, Pittsburgh Pirates, Montreal Expos, California Angels, Kansas City Royals, Chicago White Sox, Seattle Mariners, Minnesota Twins , Texas Rangers and Oakland Athletics.

I also spoke with such teams as Dallas Cowboys, Miami Dolphins, Atlanta Falcons, New Orleans Saints, San Francisco 49'ers and Los Angeles Rams, Tampa Bay Buccaneers, Green Bay Packers, Chicago Bears, Minnesota Vikings, Detroit Lions, Washington Redskins, St. Louis

Cardinals, New York Giants, Philadelphia Eagles, Oakland Raiders, and at Hawaii Pro Bowls.

Also, Cincinnati Bengals, Cleveland Browns, Houston Oilers, Pittsburgh Steelers, Kansas City Chiefs, Los Angeles Raiders, San Diego Chargers, Seattle Seahawks, Denver Broncos and received game ball, New York Jets, New England Patriots, Buffalo Bills, Indianapolis Colts, and 1987 American and National League All Star Games.

When South Carolina Governor Jim Edwards began his political career in the state Senate, he asked me to run with him for the other Senate chair. I thanked him for the offer but explained that I had a higher calling to spread the Gospel. In that capacity, I participated in Governor Edwards' inaugural activities in 1973, speaking at the church service prior to the inaugural ceremony.

Many plaques and awards have been given. My testimony has appeared in several magazines and newspapers. I praise God for all that is accomplished through my experiences.

The theme of life for Deanna and me we have found in John 9:4, "I must work the works of Him that sent me, while it is day: for the night cometh, when no man can work."

In 1975 a valuable member, Arthur Chastain, formerly lead singer with the Oakland Quartet which had sung at our meetings, joined our evangelistic team. In late 1974 God led Arthur to us with the idea of assisting with our ministry, and he joined us full-time the following January. He and Dea cut their first album of Gospel music, "One Day at a Time," that summer and a second, "Today I Followed Jesus," early in 1976. A third, "Thank You Lord", has been completed.

In addition to singing at the services where I speak, Arthur does most of the driving as we travel America in the renovated bus that serves our family as a home on wheels. Arthur's wife, Linda, interprets for the deaf on the television ministry of Citadel Square Baptist Church in

Charleston, where they make their home with their sons, Jason and David.

Another member of our team who was sent by the Lord is Dea's paternal grandmother, Mrs. A. B. (Jennie) Fowler, affectionately called "Goggie." Her husband, an engineer on the railroad for 52 years, received Christ at age 71 and died ten years later leaving behind a strong Christian testimony. I believe the prayers of Paw Paw and Goggie helped to spare my life in Vietnam and lead Dea and me to Christ.

Goggie has four sons with whom she could have lived; but she chose to join our family and serve the Lord (at age 73), traveling with us and caring for our little girls. We added an apartment to our Litchfield Beach, South Carolina, home for her. That apartment is the heart of our home, and Goggie's baking was a daily treat for us all!

Goggie went home with the Lord on Super Bowl Sunday at age 89 and was a blessing to our family for 15 years.

In 1977, Arthur, Dea, Tara, Christa, and I went to Germany at the invitation of the Army chief of chaplains to share Christ on American Army bases throughout the country. Dea and Arthur sang, and I related my Vietnam and conversion experiences 62 times during the two weeks. I also participated in some training sessions with the men. God touched the lives of many with whom we shared.

Daily the Lord gives us opportunity to tell others about His love and grace.

XX

Christian Soldier in Korea

Wherefore take unto you the whole armor of God,
that ye may be able to withstand in the evil day,
and having done all, to stand.
Ephesians 6:13 (KJV)

As the jet taxied down the runway, it seemed to me that I was re-living a somber day. The scene was the same: Charleston Airport . . . Deanna waving as I headed for some place half a world away . . . again, as a soldier; but this time it was to fight a spiritual battle as a soldier in the Army of Jesus Christ, equipped not with military weapons but with the armor of God, the "sword of the Spirit, which is the Word of God."

I was one of some twenty-five pastors, evangelists and lay workers who had been invited by Dr. E. J. Daniels to participate in an evangelistic crusade in Korea September 1-8, 1974. The event was sponsored by "Christ for the World" (Dr. Daniels' ministry based in Orlando, Florida). Lee Fisher served as music director.

For some time I had hoped and prayed for an opportunity to go back to the Orient. Tokyo was our first stop. On my first visit to Japan I saw little more than the inside of the hospital. This time I was out on the street among the people. The first time I didn't know the Lord as Savior. This time I introduced others to Him.

As we flew over the islands of Japan toward Korea I was reminded of Vietnam high mountains dipping to shoreline, many lagoons, harbors and rice paddies.

From Seoul, the capital of South Korea, we traveled to Chun Ju, where Dr. Daniels was to preach following crusades held by his team in 20 area churches simultaneously.

The Koreans extended a hearty welcome to us. Chun Ju Mayor Byung Ui Won sent a police escort to meet our team at the edge of the city, and later gave a luncheon in our honor. City officials met us in private audiences in their offices. The Honorable In Sung Hwang, governor of the province of Jeonla Bukdo, delivered the main address at a reception for our team, officially welcomed us at the opening service of the crusade, and hosted a reception for us at his mansion where we listened to the talented Korean-American vocalist, Miss Kim Wickes.

Permanently blinded by a bomb explosion in 1950 when communists invaded her village, Miss Wickes was adopted at age 10 by an American couple, Mr. and Mrs. George Wickes of Dayton, Indiana. She accepted Christ at a Billy Graham crusade in Indianapolis in 1959. Later she attended Wheaton College, earned bachelor and master's degrees in music from Indiana University where she began work on a doctoral program, and received a Fulbright Scholarship to the Vienna Institute of Music and Dramatic Arts in Austria. Kim is a gifted soloist with inspiring faith.

South Korea, without any doubt, is experiencing a modern day spiritual awakening. We awoke the first morning around 4:15 a.m. to chimes pealing out "Near the Cross" over the mountainside, calling Korean Christians to pray. Daily hundreds assembled in churches at this early hour to call upon God in prayer, sometimes all praying aloud at once. They prayed not only for their own nation to be unified under the banner of the Gospel, but also for their friends in the United States, that America might follow Jesus.

Surely the Holy Spirit prepared hearts for the crusade in Chun Ju. Total attendance for the eight days was conservatively estimated at 235,000. Some 18,400 professed to accept Christ and an estimated 10,000 more made public decisions. Dr. Daniels labeled the event "a modern Pentecost."

Being a part of this evangelistic outreach in Korea was one of the most gratifying experiences of my life. It was exciting to speak through an interpreter and share in a miracle as the Holy Spirit worked through both of us. I spoke about fifty times in schools and jails, at military bases and leper colonies, at Rotary Club and Presbyterian Hospital, and on television. I also witnessed in some rather unlikely locations on the street where a one-eyed man who lived under a bridge prayed to receive Christ; at the market place where an old man, about eighty, rejoiced to learn that he could have eternal life; on a volleyball court at a school I passed on a 4-1/2-mile run through the city . . . one youngster spoke English and interpreted as I shared the Gospel and about forty-five school children made decisions for Christ.

I felt quite at home visiting a leper colony and speaking to people who had been disfigured by the dread disease. Arriving late for the service, I found them singing praises to the Lord. Some lepers were later brought by bus from the colony for the first two crusade services; but Dr. Daniels regretfully had to discontinue the practice at the urging of local leaders, who felt that the fear of contacting leprosy might keep thousands away.

Having fought in Vietnam alongside Korean troops, I felt at home, too, on the military bases. One base had 40,000 men in training with 600 new recruits arriving each day. Our visit coincided with the dedication of a new chapel. A two-star general introduced our team and unselfishly turned over the entire program to us. After I shared my testimony before the 1500 men attending the service, Dr. John Tierany preached. About three hundred soldiers ran forward to make public decisions for Christ at the invitation.

At a private girls' school about fifteen hundred students dressed neatly in uniforms sat on the ground in the stadium listening attentively to my testimony. After the program I toured the school and marvelled at the excellent facilities. The students attend classed from 8 a.m. until 3 p.m. Punctuality is stressed. I was amazed to learn that 95 percent of the Koreans can read and write.

As I walked down the halls of that school, girls would grab my arm and pull me into their classroom. On every blackboard, written in English, were the words, "I love you." When I pointed to them and said, "I love you, too!", they clapped and smiled.

At a prison housing some two thousand inmates, 67 of the 450 at the service received Christ as Savior. The warden presented me a beautiful picture painted by one of the prisoners.

Attending a Korean Rotary Club meeting, I presented a pennant from my home club in Georgetown and received one in return. When asked to speak, I shared what Christ has meant in my life; and afterwards I invited the men to pray.

Dr. David Seale, director of the 350-bed Presbyterian Medical Center in Chun Ju, his wife, Mary, invited our team to their home for breakfast. Dr. Seale, an outstanding surgeon and cancer specialist, told us about mission work there and about the development of the hospital where I later spoke to doctors, nurses, and nursing students.

Mrs. Seale explained to us the structure of the Korean language and taught us a few simple terms. She also wrote for me a letter in Korean that I could arrange to copy at home and mail back to my Korean friends.

I have concluded that the secret to the evangelism explosion in Korea is primarily prayer- earnest petitions and praise from humble hearts. Koreans are excited about Jesus Christ. It was thrilling to see them actually run forward to accept Him as Savior.

I have thanked God many times for those exciting days in that beautiful country where our team labored for the Lord with eternal results.

Clebe and Jerry Falwell, in his office, at Thomas Road Baptist Church, Lynchburg, Virginia

Clebe McClary at Erskine College in Due West, South Carolina

XXI

FIDO

A Price to Pay

For ye are brought with a price: therefore glorify God in your body, and in your spirit, which are God's.
I Corinthians 6:20 (KJV)

The nightmare of Vietnam is not easily forgotten. The horror of that midnight on Hill 146 will never be erased. Daily I am reminded of the cost of liberty by the price that I paid 100 percent disability. Saddled with such a discouraging label, I have found it exciting to look ahead and see what can still be achieved. My motto helps FIDO — Forget it and Drive On!

Disadvantaged with only one eye and arm, I am not often disheartened; but I do at times become impatient. Pain is a constant companion; and it is invariably heightened on cold, rainy days by "phantom pains" which give the sensation that the left arm is present and should function.

I gain a sense of accomplishment by doing something with one hand that most people take for granted, such as throwing a football, shooting a basket, serving a tennis ball or baiting a hook, even though I have to hold either the hook or the cricket with my teeth!

It's the little things that are the most frustrating. It takes me longer to drive a nail, hang curtains, or put up a fence. Digging one post hole is a day's work. I don't like having to pay people to do jobs around the house that any husband should be able to do. It isn't the money that bothers me but the fact that I would like to do them myself. I still care for our lawn and operate the tractor to mow pasture and weeds.

Since my legs have recovered fully from the wounds, I run often. I also play tennis and golf. The handle of my golf club is built up like a baseball bat to give me a better grip, but occasionally it slips out of my grasp. Sometimes people attempt to "encourage" me by saying they know a one-armed person who shoots par golf. I don't shoot par golf because my right hand doesn't work too well, but I still enjoy the game.

When it comes to hunting, I'm a pretty good shot at duck, dove, and deer, but not very successful at quail shooting which requires quick reflexes. I need time to get set, balance the gun on my artificial arm or stump, them aim.

My handicap determines my style of dress to some extent. I prefer shoes that do not have to be tied and shirts that snap instead of button. When traveling alone, I sometimes have to ask the hotel maid or a guest in another room to help button my uniform. I don't particularly enjoy that; but I do not mind receiving help at times because I like to help other people, handicapped or not. I realize that many people want to help me also.

Rarely do I conclude that I cannot do something without giving it a good try, but I almost met defeat one day traveling with Jerry Falwell. By the time we stopped for lunch, I was starved and ordered a "whopper." That will humble a one-armed man! I just looked at it for a while, trying to decide where to begin. I discovered that it takes two hands to handle a whopper!

Occasionally I relive the terror of Vietnam. Once as Dea and I were eating at a sidewalk cafe in New York, a taxi backfired; and I jumped, nearly upsetting the table. During a storm I become restless as the flashes of lightning and rumbling of thunder bring back the battle memories.

I don't think my suffering was in vain. The Lord has used my experiences for good by drawing many lives to Him. It's hard to see any good that came from the war in Vietnam, but I don't believe our effort was wasted. Surely some seed was planted for Christ that cannot be stamped out.

I liked the Vietnamese people and wanted to bring a ten-year-old orphan boy home with me. "Sammy" was always around base area, and we became great friends. After learning that I was missing in action in Hai Van Pass, Sammy must have assumed I was dead; for he never came back.

Many Americans wonder if the Vietnamese really cared whether they were free or if they truly wanted the right to vote. While I was there a village outside of Da Nang held its first really free election. On voting day the Communists dropped a few mortars and rockets, killing about seven and wounding 15 or so. Still, 89.9 percent of those eligible cast their vote. In America it is not uncommon for a mere 30 percent of the eligible voters to exercise that privilege; and if the first person in line were to be shot, 30 percent wouldn't turn out. I believe the Vietnamese appreciated their freedom while they had it.

The ceasefire agreement of January 27, 1973, did not bring peace. We watched as the last glimmer of hope for liberty in South Vietnam was smothered by the Communist takeover.

A lot of people have asked my opinion of the Vietnamese refugees coming to our land which is already plagued with overcrowding and unemployment problems. My reply is that we should have won the war and given them their own farms and factories to provide for their families. Since we failed, we owe them a chance. In Vietnam today they would be persecuted, perhaps slaughtered, by the Communists. If a Vietnamese, speaking very little English and leaving behind everything he owns, obtains and keeps a job here; then he deserves it.

I believe our unemployment problem results not so much from the scarcity of jobs as from the abundance of lazy Americans who are too proud to accept jobs that are available.

While I was in Vietnam we tried to win the war. I believe we could have won it in six months if we had been turned loose to fight aggressively. You can't be a "good guy" and fight a war. Politicians can't make the most effective decisions for the military. We invested too many lives to give the country to the Communists. I personally feel that the Communists will take over the world if we don't wake up. Whether we fight them in Southeast Asia or right here at home, we will have to take a stand and pay the price to preserve the freedoms that we take for granted.

America may boast of being a free country, guaranteeing freedom of speech, press and religion; but these freedoms did not come to us free, nor were they cheap. An immeasurable price has been paid.

I once heard Paul Harvey relate a story about a group of youths who set out to get the best of a hermit noted for his wisdom. One of the boys caught a little bird which he planned to cup in his hands while challenging the old man to guess what he held. If the hermit knew that it was a bird, the boy would have him to guess if it were living or dead. If he said dead, the boy planned to open his hands and let the bird fly away; but if he said living, he would crush it with his palms. The youths rapped at the old man's door and presented the riddle.

"It seems to me you've got a bird there, my son," said the hermit.

"That's right, it's a bird," replied the youth, adding smugly, "but is it living or dead?"

The hermit looked at the boy then at his buddies and answered, "It is as you will, my son. It is as you will."

Across this country, I tell young people, "The future of America is as you will. You also hold in your hands a bird-the beautiful eagle that symbolizes liberty and freedom. You can care for it, feed and nourish it, and watch it fly; or neglect it, starve and crush it, and watch it die."

A great price was paid by the people who founded our nation. As I look to our heritage, I visualize George Washington respected as the father of our country, our first President, our first commander-in-chief-on a battlefield surrounded by his soldiers, barefooted, bleeding and suffering, but I see him on his knees. The outstanding leaders of our history who paid a price for freedom have been spiritual men who also paid a price to follow Jesus.

American's progress has far surpassed the other areas of the world settled long before our land. But we are still a needy people. Our nation's greatest need today is to turn back to God, who promised in II Chronicles 7:14, "If my people, which are called by my name, shall humble themselves, and pray, and seek my face, and turn their wicked ways; then will I hear from heaven, and will forgive their sin, and will heal their land."

Joshua declared, "As for me and my house, we will serve the Lord," America needs men and women who will take such a stand, who will make time for daily family devotions, and who will speak out boldly for the Lord Jesus Christ.

A recent national survey revealed that the average adult in America spends three minutes a day talking to their young people. Dr. James Dobson says that the average middle aged, middle class daddy says he spends 40 minutes a day with his children, but actual tests show that he spends 37.75 seconds a day! That is a poor average and hardly sufficient to fulfil Paul's instruction to bring up our children "in the nurture and admonition of the Lord."

I do not know the author of the poem, "Don't Blame the Children," but it seems to hit home in America.

Don't blame the children when they are found
Drinking and gambling and running around.
If by their conduct they bring you shame
Is it the children or us parents to blame?
Where are your children, your pride and your joy?
Where is your girl and where is your boy?
If by their conduct they bring you shame,
Is it the children or us parents to blame?
We read in the papers and hear on the air
Of killing and stealing and crime everywhere.
We sigh and we say as we notice a trend,
Man, this younger generation, where will it end?
But can we be sure that it's their fault alone,
That maybe a part of it isn't our own?
Too much money to spend, too much idle time,
Too many movies of passion and crime,
Too many books not fit to be read,
Too much evil in what they hear said,
Too many children encouraged to roam
By too many parents that won't stay home.
Kids don't make the liquor; they don't run the bars.
They don't make the laws and they don't buy the cars.
They don't sell the drugs the first time that idle the brain;
It's all done by us older folks, greedy for gain.
Delinquent teenagers, O how we condemn
The sins of a nation and blame it on them.
By the rule of the blameless the Good Book makes known;
Who is among us to cast the first stone?
In how many cases we find that it's true
This label delinquent fits us older folks, too.

I once heard Bart Starr, coach of the Green Bay Packers, say, "Commitment is the name of the game." A former Packers receiver, Carroll Dale, whom I met when speaking to the Packers team a few years ago, had greatly impressed me with his commitment to the Lord.

Carroll was once quoted as saying, "Our power of influence is not necessarily in what we say, but in how we live under daily pressures."

Bill Forrester, former linebacker for the Green Bay Packers and teammate of Carroll Dale, wrote to me. "Mental toughness" are two words used by Coach Vince Lombardi to mold championship football teams. You have shown more mental toughness than anyone I have ever known."

I am what I am because of being associated first with Christ Jesus in a personal way and second, because I have associated with Christians who truly put Christ first in their lives. Lee and Betty Fisher have been an inspiration to me. God gave Lee the beloved song, "The Christ of Every Crisis." After his retirement from the Billy Graham Evangelistic Association, Lee and Betty went to Guatemala to assist with the rebuilding of homes destroyed by the earthquake. One of Lee's poems is "A Careful Man." I subtitle it "A Careful Marine" and adapt it accordingly, with Lee's permission.

A careful Marine I want to be, a little fellow follows me.
I do not care to go astray, for fear he may go the selfsame way.
I cannot once escape his eye, what e'er he sees me do he'll try.
Like me he says he's going to be, this little lad who follows me.
He thinks that I am big and fine, believes in every word of mine

The base in me he must not see, this little lad who
follows me.
I must remember as I go through summer suns and
winter snows,
I'm building for the years to be this little lad who
follows me.

We're building that son or daughter, that child on our street or block; we're their Bobby Richardson, Bart Starr, Roger Stauback, Paul Anderson, Jerry Clower, Tom Landry, Grant Teaff, Lester Roloff, Tim Lee, Josh McDowell, James Dobson, Chuck Swindoll, Ken Hatfield, Harold Morris, Miss Bertha Smith and Hans Tanzler. We have eyes looking up at us, little people wanting to live their lives exactly as we do. We need to consider seriously how we are influencing those lives.

Bobby Richardson's father had a tombstone business. As a child, Bobby carved into a discarded piece of granite a well know quotation he had seen on a plaque. When his father died in 1963, that quotation was engraved on his tombstone. It goes like this:

Only one life, 't will soon be past;
Only what's done for Christ will last.

Clebe and Bobby Richardson

XXII

Giving What It Takes

If any man will come after me, let him deny himself, and take up his cross, and follow me. For whosoever will save his life shall lose it: and whosoever will lose his life for my sake shall find it. For what is a man profited, if he shall gain the whole world, and lose his own soul? Or what shall a man give in exchange for his soul?

Matthew 16:24-26 (KJV)

To God belongs the glory for the lives touched through my witness. I would like to share the experiences of two men who write from vastly different circumstances one from a mayor's office, the other from a state prison. Their stories illustrate clearly the truth penned by Paul in Act 2:21," . . . whosoever shall call on the name of the Lord shall be saved."

Hans Tanzler, Jr. mayor of Jacksonville, Florida, describes what happened October 1, 1974, at a prayer breakfast in his city.

"I was privileged to hear your inspirational testimony for Christ and to be personally touched and inspired. You gave me the strength, the inspiration and the guidance to put my hand in the hand of the Man from Galilee, as the song goes. While there were tears in my eyes when I left, there was strength in my soul and in my heart for having had my faith in Christ reaffirmed. When God decided to spare your life on that remote hill in Vietnam, He unquestionably had in mind that because of what you had experienced, you could be a more effective servant of His will. I personally have never met a more effective and persuasive inspirational disciple of the Christian faith than you. I only hope that you can be half as effective in changing the lives of others as you were in changing the life of the mayor of Jacksonville."

Harold Morris graduated from Winyah High School in 1959, a year ahead of me. He was captain of the football, basketball and baseball teams during his senior year and was chosen the most outstanding athlete in all sports. He is now paroled and pardoned from Georgia State prison, serving a double life sentence for armed robbery and murder, having been implicated by two other men in a crime which I'm convinced he did not commit.

On February 11, 1974, I visited Harold at the prison near Reidsville, Georgia, and talked with him about his relationship with the Lord. I left a Bible with him and later brought Deanna to meet him. She gave Harold a cassette tape of my testimony and asked him to read these Scriptures: Philippians 1:3, I John 1:9: I Peter 2:24, Roman 6:23 and Revelation 3:20.

"Clebe loves you and I love you," she told him. "We're going to pray for you. God's going to help you."

In his room that night, Harold played the tape over and over and read the verses. Finally he sank to his knees, begging God for forgiveness of his sins and receiving Christ as Savior. Several months later he was chosen to participate in a prison-sponsored program in which he speaks to high schools, churches and civic organizations about the horrors of prison and the change that Christ has made in his life. During the first year, he spoke to over 15,000 students and adults. In January, 1977, the Reidsville Jaycees presented him with the Jaycees Presidential Award of Honor for his contribution to the youth of the Reidsville community.

Harold shares, "Hundreds of youths have written to me for advice. Frequently a young person confides that my testimony has helped him to straighten out his life. I honestly would not trade that for anything-not even my freedom. I don't ask God to get me out of prison. I try to live one day at a time, trusting Him and thanking Him for all that He has already done. I believe He has a purpose for my life. I owe my life to Him.

"I was a lost sinner at the end of my rope, ready to take my own life, when Clebe and Deanna introduced me to the Savior who died for my sins. On the day that the judge pronounced my sentence, I stopped living. But on the day that God erased the penalty of my sins when Christ came into my heart, I began to live a new creature.

"I shall always be indebted to Clebe and Deanna for putting love in my heart by leading me to the Author of love Jesus Christ. If they can do it for me, a convict serving a double life sentence for armed robbery and murder, they can do it for others by leading them to the same Lord and Savior, Jesus Christ."

A mayor, a prisoner, a Marine . . . God has a purpose for each life.

My definition of a successful person is one who knows God and His plan for his life and strives to achieve it. If God can use a shot-up, one-armed Marine like me, think of what He could do for others. He is a God of miracles; I'm living proof.

One of the greatest stories to come out of Vietnam belongs to a good friend of mine, Lieutenant Bruce Bickel, a graduate of the U. S. Naval Academy who is now director of the Fellowship of Christian Athletes ministry in Chicago.

Lieutenant Bickel arrived in Vietnam just before the Tet offensive in 1968. After 9,000 civilians were slaughtered by the enemy at Hue, our forces recaptured the city and set up orphanages. Lieutenant Bickel was involved in the work. One of the facilities housing 32 boys, ages four to thirteen, was hit by an enemy mortar attack. An eight-year-old boy was severely wounded and was rushed to the hospital, where he needed a blood transfusion.

The lieutenant wanted to give blood; but his type did not have the immunity that a Vietnamese person's does, so he went back to the orphanage to explain to those children that their friend was going to die unless one of them gave blood. A six-year-old named Kai raised his hand and said, "Me, I give."

He was rushed by jeep to the hospital, laid on a stretcher by his friend and prepared for the transfusion. A little while after the needle was inserted into his arm, Kai started to whimper. Lieutenant Bickel walked over and asked, "Son, what's wrong? Does it hurt?" Kai gave no reply. A little later, he began to cry severely. Lieutenant Bickel asked again, "Kai, what's wrong? Are you scared? Does the needle hurt your arm?" The little six-year-old boy giving blood to save his friend's life looked up at the lieutenant and said, "How long will it take me to die?"

Kai had never heard of a transfusion. He didn't know he just gave a little blood . . . he thought he gave it all. He was willing to give all of his blood so that his friend might live.

A greater sacrifice Christ made at Calvary His blood to redeem lost mankind . . . His life that we might live.

One of the men in my platoon had engraved on his cigarette lighter:

"You have never lived until you have nearly died."

That doesn't mean much to most people; it didn't mean much to me, either, until I nearly died; but I learned there is a tragedy worse than physical death: it is spiritual death.

Romans declares, "All have sinned and come short of the glory of God" (3:23). "The wages of sin is death, but the gift of God is eternal life through Jesus Christ our Lord" (6:23).

Jesus said, "And whosoever liveth and believeth in me shall never die . . . " (John 11:26).

In early April, 1977, nine years after that night of terror on Hill 146, I was invited to Haltom City, Texas, to speak in a Baptist Church. As I stepped off the plane at Dallas-Fort Worth Airport, I saw him . . . the man who saved my life, Bob Lucas.

For a minute we just stood there. Then our arms were around each other. It was too deep for a handshake.

I had talked once by phone with Lucas, who was a policeman in Haltom City. When he saw a leaflet announcing my coming to North Richland Hills Baptist Church, just a block from his home, he decided to meet the plane. We played tennis and reminisced. I learned that Luke, who had earlier received the Silver Star, turned down a medal for what he did for me. He said simply, "It was my job." It was my life. In a way, the favor was returned. Deanna led his wife to the Lord, in whom she found new life.

Of all the honors that I have received, the most meaningful presentation was a plaque sent to me at Philadelphia Naval Hospital by the men in my platoon. It bears the quotation I learned from Coach Red Myers at Erskine printed on cardboard then hung on the wall of my hootch in Vietnam:

"In this world of give and take, there are not enough people who are willing to give what it takes."

Believe in the Lord Jesus Christ. That's all that it takes. Surrender to Christ is not at all defeat but 100% victory!

The Ballad of Clebe McClary

Tune to Anybody Here Seen my old Friend
Words by Our Pastor Bob Barrows
Pawleys Island Baptist Church
Son of Cliff Barrows — Billy Graham Team

1. Was a man from Carolina,
Clebe McClary was his name.
Born way down in Georgetown County,
From Scotch-Irish stock he came.
Grew up on a big plantation
Mother Jessie, she raised three
Cap'n Pat, he kept them mindin',
sometimes on his bended knee

Chorus Has anybody here seen Clebe McClary?
Last I saw he's runnin out the door
If you ask him, "Clebe, why are you runnin?"
He'll smile and say, "I'm runnin for my Lord!"

2. Met up with a girl, Deanna,
Chose to take her for his own.
But soon he heard his country callin'
Vietnam was now his home.
Round his men the guns were firing,
An explosion ripped the air.
Soon he felt his body flyin'
But the Lord, Clebe's life He spared.

3. Coming home to his Deanna,
Body broken, spirit strong
Tough old Clebe, he started mendin'
Through the pain his faith grew long
Well, I guess they've had some hard times
And disappointments on the way.
But the Lord knew what He's doin'

And now He uses Clebe each day.
4. And God's blessed him with a family,
Tara, Christa, Goggie too.
And now Clebe, he tells his story
From here to there to Tim-buck-too!

Deanna, Christa, Tara and Clebe in front of their home church, Pawleys Island Baptist Church

What is a Grandmother?

Written by a 9-year-old girl

A grandmother is a lady who has no children of her own.
She likes other people's girls and boys.
A grandfather is a man grandmother.
He goes for walks with the boys
and they talk about fishing and stuff like that.
Grandmothers don't have to do anything except to be there.
They're old so they shouldn't have to play hard or run.
It is enough if they drive us to the market
where the pretend horse is and have lots of dimes ready.
When they take us for walks they slow down past things
like pretty leaves and caterpillars and they never say "hurry up."
Usually grandmothers are fat, but not too fat to tie your shoes.
They wear glasses and funny underwear.
They can take their teeth and gums off.
Grandmothers don't have to be smart,
only answer questions like,
"Why isn't God married?" and "How come dogs chase cats?"
Everybody should try to have a grandmother,
especially if you don't have television.
Because grandmothers are the only grown-ups who have time.

Deanna's grandmother, "Goggie" Fowler
with a young Tara and Christa. Goggie always had time for us.

Clebe McClary at Billy Graham Crusade, on National TV, at Angel Stadium in Annaheim, California

Special Olympics, Columbia, South Carolina, May 14, 1987
From left to right, S.L. Toney, Cpl., Mike Lanier, Lt. Clebe McClary, USMC (Ret), Sgt. Jim Braddock, Chief Richard Ruonala, Governor Carroll A. Campbell, Jr., South Carolina Governor, Eunice Kennedy Schriver, Chairperson U.S. Special Olympics

Clebe and Deanna McClary, 25th wedding anniversary, March 26, 1992

(Rick Smoak Photo)

Above: *Clebe speaking to a battalion from South Carolina in Honduras*
Below: *Col. Jim Wilson and Clebe, USMC, in Panama*

Clebe at the Killing Fields, October 31, 1990, Cambodia

Clebe running across Cambodia and Vietnam, November, 1990

Christa with Chesty
Photo Vern Verna

Tara and Clebe,
Miss South Carolina Pageant.
Tara is a 1992 graduate
of Furman University.

Deanna, Deanna's mother, Mrs. Dean Fowler, and Tara

Clebe and Christa on her wedding day
April 28, 1996

Clebe and Deanna with Christa and Tara on Christa's wedding day.

Christa and John cut the delicious cake by Edibile Arts, Raleigh, North Carolina.

Clebe and son-in-law Dr. John McElveen, at a Duke game

Teresa Dearr Photography

McElveen Family Portrait

Anderson Photography, Charleston, SC

John holding John Thomas, Dr. William Willemon
and Christa holding Madeline
at the twins' dedication service at Duke Chapel

Teresa Dearr Photography

John Thomas and Madeline

Teresa Dearr Photography

Madeline Bonneau McElveen
Future Miss Clemson?

Teresa Dearr Photography

John Thomas and Madeline

A McClary Family Portrait, 2000

The twins' first Easter at Pawleys

Nannie and her first great grandson, John Thomas

Nannie with her "girls" Christa, Deanna and Tara

Dr. Conyers O'Bryan, on behalf of
Gov. David Beasley, presents
The Order of the Palmetto Award to Clebe

Dean Fowler, Jr. (Deanna's brother) with Clebe and Deanna

Clebe with good friend, former SC Governor David Beasley

Deanna and Clebe catching up with
Senator Strom Thurmond at a USC game

Clebe with Marvin Bass, former head coach at USC (Dan Reeves' college coach) and presently one of the Falcon coaches

Clebe with four-time Pro Bowl linebacker, Jessie Tuggle

Clebe and record-setting Falcon kicker, Morten Andersen

After the Falcons/Saints game Clebe caught up with Florida Heisman trophy winner and Saints quarterback, Danny Wuerffel

Clebe and Deanna with Mike Trout and Dr. James Dobson during their Focus on the Family broadcast in May 1998

Clebe and Dr. James Dobson pheasant hunting at the Paul Nelson farm in Gettysburg, South Dakota

Clebe and Bobby Richardson at a South Carolina Fellowship of Christian Athletes event

Clebe and the "rebel with a cause," Franklin Graham, in Boone, NC

Before speaking to the Cadets, Clebe meets with friend General John Grinalds at the Citadel

Clebe with long-time friend Ike Bullard and General Carl Mundy, former Commandant, USMC, in Charleston, SC

What an honor to meet Colonel Wes Fox with the Virginia Tech Corps of Cadets

More of our country's best.
Deanna and Clebe with General "Fig" Newton and his wife Elouise at Randolph AFB, San Antonio, TX

Clebe and Mark Jones of Midland, TX with Cooper Henderson of Artesia, New Mexico, one of the winningest high school football coaches in America

Clebe with former Tennessee standout and Colts quarterback, Peyton Manning

Good friend. Great coach. Clebe with
Bobby Bowden of the Florida State Seminoles

Another coaching legend. Clebe with
Gene Stallings, former Alabama head coach

Clebe with good friend Jerry Horne

Clebe with friend Al Hartley, creator of the Archie *comics*

Clebe with Craig Wierda and his son, Drew Wierda, on their boat and hunting in South Dakota

Deanna's brother Dean Fowler, Jr. and his wife Gail

Clebe visiting with his Aunt Juliet Jones in San Antonio

Nannie and her "hip" doctor, Dr. Del Schutte, the surgeon who performed her successful hip replacement surgery and Deanna's as well

Even hip replacement surgery and a crutch won't keep Deanna from taking a walk on the beach. Her surgery was a complete success!

Visiting with good friends,
Cindy and Tom Caradine of Birmingham, AL

Clebe and his sons-in-law,
Lee Reeves (left) and John McElveen (right)

Harold Morris visits Clebe in his Pawleys Island office

Clebe with long-time friends
Tom Lester and "the Goosehunter,"
James Hamblin of Montross, VA

Clebe and Christa with Dr. and Mrs. Jack Hough,
dear friends from Oklahoma

Friends - some of life's greatest treasures.
Clebe and Deanna with Polly and Andy Andrews

Celebrating Katie Foley's wedding with her proud father,
Tim Foley, of Tavares, Florida

Proud father Clebe on Tara's wedding day,
September 19, 1998

All wedding photographs by Tom and Florance Anderson, Charleston, SC

Mr. and Mrs. Michael Lee Reeves

The wedding cast. All precious people. We were blessed by each attendant!

Pam and Dan Reeves -
so proud of their son and new daughter!

Deanna and Clebe -
so proud of our daughter and new son!

Clebe with Lee's father, Dan and Karen and Linzy Washington, a tremendous husband and wife singing team that entertained at Tara and Lee's reception.

"Tender Warriors" - Tom Caradine, Stu Weber and Clebe at Tara and Lee's reception

Dan, Tara and Lee Reeves celebrating Tara's birthday, October 22 in Atlanta

Tara with her special men: Lee, Clebe, Daddy Do and cousin Edward

Tara and Lee

Proud Grandpa with Madeline and John Thomas on the beach at Pawleys Island.

Clebe enjoying the role of Grandpa – even grandkids won't slow him down

Lee and Tara with twins, Caroline Fraley and Daniel Cleburne at their christening in October, 2001

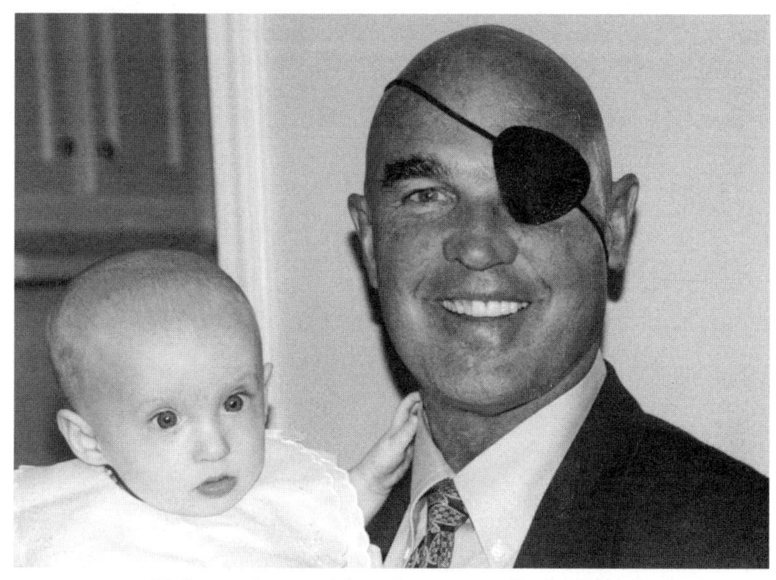

Clebe and granddaughter, Caroline Reeves

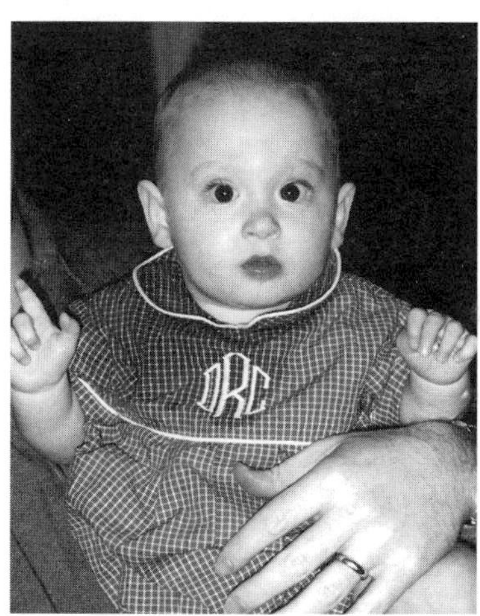

Daniel Cleburne Reeves

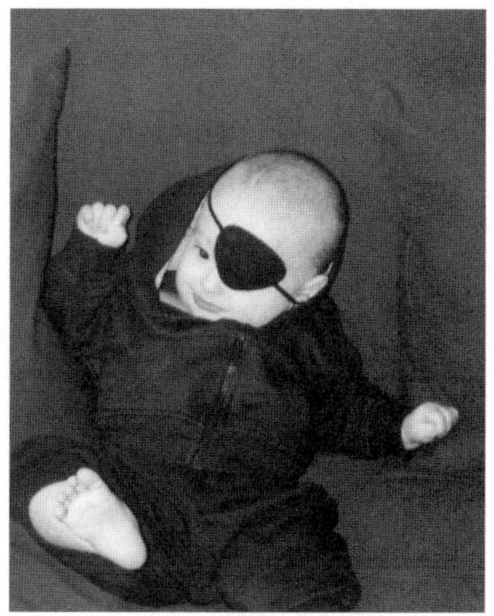

Daniel Cleburne –
the littlest pirate

Clebe and Deanna celebrated their 35th wedding anniversary in 2002 – and Deanna is still as beautiful as ever.

Clebe is proud to call President George W. Bush a friend and brother in Christ. Keep the President and Mrs. Bush in your prayers as they seek God's wisdom in leading our great country.

At the 2002 National Coaches Convention, Clebe with the "Master Coaches" –

Catching up with Texas A & M coach, R. C. Slocum at the National Coaches Convention in San Antonio

Clebe enjoying a reunion with Jule Sweat, one of his boyhood sports heroes from Winyah High School in Georgetown, SC, who went on to a great career in college ball.

Clebe at the National Coaches Convention with Fellowship of Christian Athletes president, Dal Shealy and Christian recording artist, Clifton Jansky, who was voted Newcomer of the Year by the Christian Music Association.

Clebe enjoying a break with University of Miami coach Larry Coker and his lovely wife.

What an honor to visit again with Bob Stoops, coach of the 2000 National Championship Team at Oklahoma University

Clebe congratulating former Oklahoma coach Barry Switzer the night he was inducted into the College Football Hall of Fame.

Clebe with North Carolina Tarheel standout, Ronald Curry.

General Ralph "Ed' Eberhart, who was appointed in 2002 by President George W. Bush to be the Northern Commander of Homeland Defense. Outstanding leader. A man of great courage and character, it's good to know we have men like him in charge.

It was an honor to meet General and Mrs. John Handy of the U.S. Air Force. Another one of America's best, giving what it takes to make this country great.

Clebe visiting long-time friend and Cheraw, SC native, Fisher DeBerry, head coach at the U.S. Air Force Academy in Colorado Springs, Colorado.

Clebe with another good friend and terrific coach, Jerry Moore, head football coach at Appalachian State University.

Clebe enjoying some time with good friends from Atlanta, Charles and Kay Reeves.

Clebe at a Christian businessmen's breakfast in Myrtle Beach with Pawleys Island neighbor Pete DiVenere and guest speaker Atlanta Falcons coach Dan Reeves.

Clebe and Deanna love visiting in the home of good friends Pete and Barbara Hanna of Birmingham, Alabama.

What a privilege to be with David Jeremiah at Shadow Mountain Community Church in California.

Deanna posing in her official uniform as a participant in the 2002 Winter Olympics Torch Run.

Clebe with Dwight Clark, Clemson grad and former San Francisco 49er, now Director of Football Operations with the Cleveland Browns. Dwight is famous for "The Catch" he made off a Joe Montana pass to beat the Dallas Cowboys in the 1981 NFC Championship game.

Clebe with Jerry Butler, former All-American at Clemson, now with the Cleveland Browns.

Clebe speaking at a function with Vice President Dick Cheney.

Clebe and Deanna enjoying a visit from Texas governor, Rick Perry.

Clebe and Deanna gear up for a windy trip around San Francisco bay with Chaplain Don Biadog of the U.S. Coast Guard and Oscar and Barbara Munoz. Oscar and Clebe remain good friends from their "Texas Pete" days in Vietnam.

Clebe with another Vietnam buddy, Mike Harder, on a speaking trip to Hawaii.

Texas native Henry Covarrubias was on his first patrol with Clebe on that fateful night in Vietnam.

Clebe and Deanna are always happy to see Billy "Z" Zeoli, president of Gospel Film Productions in Michigan.

Clebe and Deanna with three men who changed the course of their lives, from left to right: Sam Anderson, who counseled with them the night they accepted Christ, Billy Zeoli, the evangelist who preached the message and Bobby Richardson, the former Yankee great who shared his testimony that evening.

SUCCESS

See

U you

Communicate

Commitment

Enthusiasm

Start

S.T.P. (Sustain the pace)

PIG

Professionalism
Integrity
Guts

CLEBE McCLARY MISSION STATEMENT:

1. **Do Right**
2. **Don't Screw Up**
3. **Finish Strong**

TEAM

Together
Everyone
Accomplishes
More

PRIDE

P*ersonal*
R*esponsibility*
I*n*
D*aily*
E*ffort*

BIONIC

Believe

It

Or

Not,

I

Care

PATCH

Positive
Attitude
That
Characterizes
Hope

FIDO

FORGET IT -
DRIVE ON

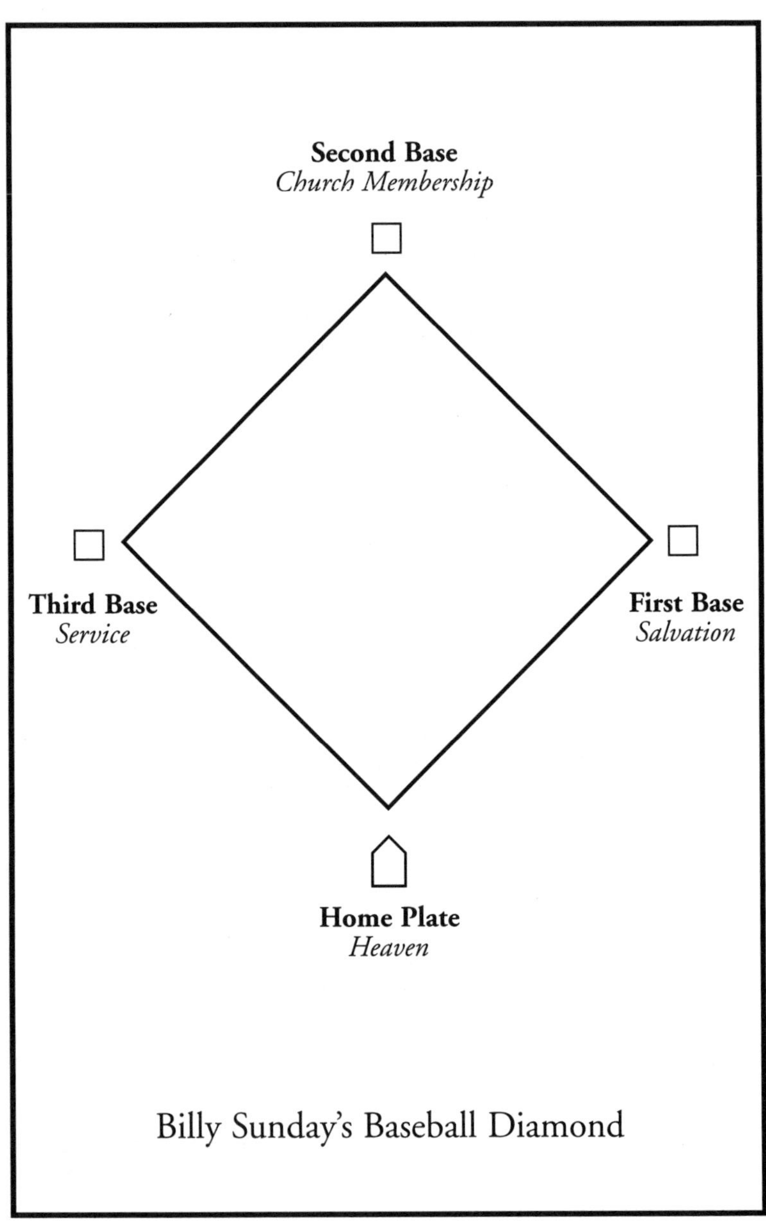

In the 1924 World Series between the Washington Senators and the New York Giants, Senator left-fielder Goose Goslin was called out at home for failing to touch first base.

Clebe has always said he's "ready to go." Modeling his "box" for the man who made it, Dr. Lynn Tipton of Elizabethhton, TN. Clebe's "box" is on display in his office as a reminder that time is short and he "must work the works of Him that sent me."

In this world of give and take, there are not enough people willing to give what it takes–

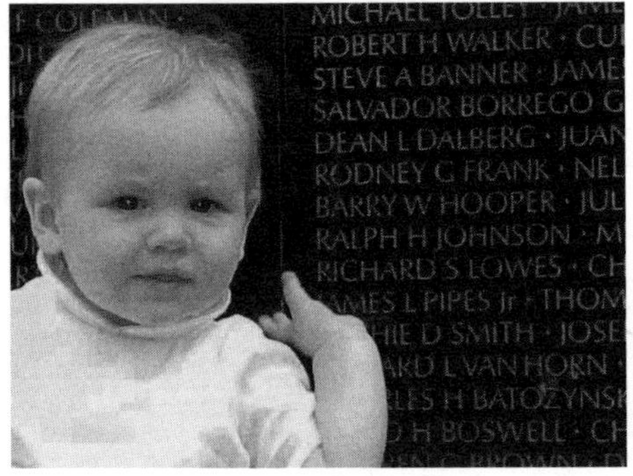

Grandson John Thomas McElveen visiting the Vietnam Wall Memorial in Washington, DC

Many gave a lot... These gave it all.

Thank you for taking the time to read my story. If I can be of service to you or your organization, contact me at:

Clebe McClary
P. O. Box 535
Pawleys Island, SC 29585
(843) 237-2582 Phone
(843) 237-1890 Fax
email: clebe@clebemcclary.net
web: clebemcclary.net

Clebe McClary is a living example of "Giving what it takes." As a Certified Speaking Professional he has spoken in all 50 states and 30 foreign countries. Clebe has conquered adversity to become one of America's most sought after speakers. His message of courage, determination and dedication will compel you to soar beyond the limit.